The Federal
Government
and Higher
Education

The Federal
Government
and Higher
Education

♦ The American Assembly
Columbia University

Englewood Cliffs, N. J.
PRENTICE-HALL, INC. *1960*

Preface

For each new subject taken up by The American Assembly, it is the custom to begin discussions with a national meeting at Arden House, Harriman, New York, and to follow this with regional, state and municipal Assemblies.

This volume, edited by Douglas M. Knight, is the required background reading for all meetings of the Seventeenth American Assembly, whether at Arden House or elsewhere. It is designed as well for the general reading public.

The conclusions of The Arden House Assembly are found in this volume beginning on page 193.

The Assembly is grateful to Carnegie Corporation of New York for a generous grant for the entire Seventeenth Assembly program. However, the Corporation is not to be understood as approving by virtue of its grant any of the views expressed in this book. Nor does The American Assembly, a non-partisan educational organization, take an official stand. The views are the authors' own.

Henry M. Wriston
President
The American Assembly

77165

Contents

INTRODUCTION

Challenge and Dilemma in Higher Education   1

Douglas M. Knight, *Editor*

1   Purpose and Policy in Higher Education   6

Douglas M. Knight

The National Setting, 7
Education at its Best, 9
The Idea of Excellence, 13
Confusion and Clarity in Higher Education, 18
Problems of Policy, 21

2   Federal Policies and Practices in Higher Education   29

Charles A. Quattlebaum

Chronological Summary, 31
Origin of Federal Policy, 34
Constitutional Background, 35
Education for National Defense, 36
Early Federal Grants Policy, 42
Education in Special Federal Jurisdictions, 43
Contracts with Colleges for Research, 44

Land-Grant Colleges and Associated Services, 44
The Role of the Office of Education, 46
Vocational Education and Rehabilitation, 48
Education for Veterans, 50
Surplus Property Disposal, 51
Depression-Period Programs and Policies, 53
Recommendations of Advisory Commissions, 53
Policies in International Education, 58
Scholarships, Fellowships, Traineeships, 60
College Housing Programs, 61
Other Historical Policies and Programs, 62
Current Policies and Programs, 63
Conclusions, 71

3 Federal Sponsorship of University Research 76

James McCormack and Vincent A. Fulmer

The Universities and the Federal Government, 77
The Role of University Research, 79
Project Selection and Administration, 87
Research Centers, 90
Secrecy in Research, 93
Publications, 98
People and Programs, 100
The Problem of Indirect Costs, 107
Capital Requirements, 118
University Participation in Government Policy Making, 130
Strengthening American Science and Engineering, 133

4 Issues in Federal Aid to Higher Education 140

John A. Perkins and Daniel W. Wood

Why Consider Federal Aid?, 140
Where can the money come from?, 144

Issues To Be Faced, 158
Stumbling Blocks to Direct Federal Support, 162
Problems of Distribution, Organization and Political Philosophy, 165
A Possible Organization for a Democracy, 173

5 National Goals and Federal Means   176

Douglas M. Knight

The Present Problem, 177
The Need for Order, 177
The Task of Cooperation, 181
Five Kinds of Planning, 184
Dangers and Dilemmas, 187
The Nation's Need, 190

Final Report of the Seventeenth American Assembly   193

Participants in the Seventeenth American Assembly   200

The American Assembly   205

The Federal
Government
and Higher
Education

Introduction:

Challenge and dilemma
in higher education

♦ Douglas M. Knight
Editor

The temerity of writing a brief book on this subject is exceeded only by the necessity of it. None of us would pretend for a moment that we could do justice to that common ground of government and higher education which is so confused and yet so critical a part of our national life. The very confusion, however, calls for discussion—and discussion which is simultaneously critical and sympathetic. Too many programs of genuine urgency are being successfully carried on to allow any of us the luxury of scorn; but too many plans are in part the result of political expediency and compromise to allow us the comfort of knowing where the relationships of the federal government and higher education are headed. We realize that a large amount of federal income is being invested in higher education of one kind and another; but we know surprisingly little beyond this fact.

1

◆ DOUGLAS M. KNIGHT, president of Lawrence College, is a former professor of English at Yale. He served on the Yale President's Committee on General Education and on the Faculty Study Fellowship program of The Fund for the Advancement of Education.

In 1954-55 he was consultant in the humanities for the American Association of Colleges for Teacher Education. He has served on the Commission on Colleges and Universities of the North Central Association of Colleges and Secondary Schools, and on the Commission on Liberal Education of the Association of American Colleges. He is a member of the Problems and Policies Committee of The American Council on Education.

Currently Dr. Knight is representing the Association of American Colleges on the National Commission on Accrediting.

Those of us involved in writing this book are by no means detached observers of the problem. Each of us, in his own way, is deeply involved in the dilemmas and benefits of federal support to higher education. At the same time, none of us approaches his task with any sense of *a priori* judgment about what the complex relationship between the two should be. In fact, all of us feel that the issues we must discuss have perhaps suffered in recent years from an overdose of prior judgment. Our common conviction is that American education must have the resources it needs to do its job in the years ahead. We are persuaded that as a nation we cannot let education drift while we play politics or argue an irrelevant principle. We must ask the painful questions of national policy and priority, knowing that we can do no more than introduce our subject. At best we can write "the prologue to a prologue."

The present revolution in higher education has too often been called a crisis; it is too important for that urgent but shallow word, since it involves three tremendous developments in the position of higher education within our total society. The first, of course, is a vast increase in the numbers of young people who expect an education beyond high school. This part of our revolution has been underway since well before 1900; there is nothing new about the problem of crowded facilities and undersized teaching staffs; the new thing has been our recognition of the

2

problem, and our understanding of the speed with which it may compound its difficulties within the next ten years. We really face a dual increase: in the number of young people of college age, and in the percentage of them who plan to go to college. These two curves of increase are at a point where they are likely to compound one another, possibly with a few years of almost violent growth.

There is a second aspect of our revolution in education, however, which has received much less attention than it deserves even though it has been with us for the last hundred years. This is a radical increase in knowledge itself—an increase of both fact and concept, which shows itself in the expanding and increasingly complex college curriculum, and which is equally evident in the strain it puts on everything from library resources to qualified faculty to the basic issue of intellectual community itself.

We shall obviously be under great stress from both these forces in the years just ahead; and we must recognize, as a result, that in this book we ask our questions about the relations of higher education and the federal government not from a base of stability in the colleges and universities, but from a base of constant and often almost uncontrolled change.

But the problems of relationship are even more acute for government at every level than for the colleges. The city and its public schools or the state and its universities face problems of finance, operation, and policy which suggest some of the areas of complication we are to encounter at the federal level.

Only some, however; the great but "ordinary" pressures of decision and operation which are put on a city or a state do not begin to define the difficulties we face when looking for a coherent and effective national policy for education. The federal government must deal with both publicly and privately controlled institutions, both secular and church-related ones. All of those with whom it works have other constituencies to satisfy; any governmental policy for higher education should theoretically be acceptable to religious hierarchies, conservative industrialists, and the legislatures of "impoverished" states. And (most obvious but most difficult of all) it should be acceptable to a Senate and House of Representatives, many of whose members have at the moment only a tangential concern for the future of higher education. It is small wonder that so much educational legislation is passed in piecemeal form, or seems to have its eyes turned in another direction—as in the case of the National Defense Education Act of 1958. Otherwise our national conflicts of judgment might assure the failure of any legislation attempted.

At the same time we recognize more and more clearly that the needs of the country cannot be satisfied by our past and oblique interest in education. Behind a study like the one we are attempting here stands something far more important than the question of what the federal government can, should, or might do in the field of higher education in the near future. We are really concerned with the question of what national policy is best for higher education itself. That national policy may or may not be dominantly expressed in governmental policy. Almost certainly we can meet the country's need only through the most thoughtful kind of cooperation among the various and deeply committed sources of power, influence and support which higher education now has available to it. It is clear, of course, that the large issues which will underlie the discovery of a coherent national policy are not our insistent or explicit concern in this book; but we hope to make our own minor contribution to them, not only through the discussions which this text will introduce, but also through the manner in which the book itself has been organized.

It is predicated above all on the assumption that higher education and the federal government can only be wisely related to one another if both of them reflect true national policy—not just a piecemeal interest by government in some specific, perhaps transient, need of higher education. Before we can describe this national policy, furthermore, we must ask some basic questions of the colleges and universities. They are under enough pressure at the moment so that they face certain genuine threats to their identity; and it is worth asking, as a result, what that corporate identity is and what it rests on in the way of basic meaning and purpose.

The first chapter seeks, then, to establish an identity for higher education, some firm image which can at least be half-discerned behind the flickering and partial efforts of any given moment. The second chapter sets in balance against this general analysis a highly specific account of the history and present state of federal action which relates in one way or another to the practice of higher education. It is the purpose of this chapter to display the many-sided nature of the federal enterprise, which is diverse not only in its origins and its purposes but equally in its administration.

So complex a congeries of programs cannot be understood, however, merely as they issue from the hands of Congress. In practice they assume significance and create problems which were no direct concern of their initiators. They exert an influence on institutions; they may at times affect educational policy in ways and in areas quite alien to their original intent. This living and organic quality of some of our present forms of federal policy is the concern of Chapter 3, which seeks to evoke what is being accomplished for both good and evil by current practice. Given the dynamic nature of these present programs, and the very large amounts of money invested in some of them, it is logical to ask next what issues of the next few years are likely to be most urgent for us in college and university operation. If Chapter 3 describes the problems implicit in some of our present programs, Chapter 4 would extend it by describing the urgent and national problem which will exist for higher education in the immediate future. There is no doubt that the needs described in this chapter must somehow be met by the country: can they be met without the greatly increased participation of the federal government? If they cannot, can federal means be devised for meeting them without the creation of impossible difficulties either of policy or of administration? To these and similar questions Chapter 4 is directed.

These difficult questions stem from the immediacies of our national situation; they must be faced if we are to keep colleges and universities functioning properly in the years ahead. There exists beyond them, however, a further range of issues which base themselves in the fundamental questions of our national policy. These issues are of two chief kinds: first, the questions of national purpose which, like many research problems of the moment, can only be answered by colleges and universities; and second, the questions of obvious and permanent educational purpose which may need to be carried out in a more effective, influential or far-reaching way than ever before. These and related questions are dealt with in a concluding chapter.

It is evident enough that within these major divisions we cannot pretend to a "complete" treatment of our subject; but perhaps a claim to this kind of finished quality would be a little dangerous in the exploration of questions which must occupy all of us so strenuously in the next few years. It will satisfy us if we contribute in some measure to the understanding of what the questions truly are, and of what must be done if we are to answer them in any abiding way.

1.

Purpose and policy in higher education

◆ DOUGLAS M. KNIGHT

If we are to think clearly about higher education and national policy, we must begin by giving it some local habitation, some name and nature. If we do not, we shall talk a good deal of nonsense about relationships between the government and the colleges. Such would not have been the case, perhaps, if this book had been written 30 or even 20 years ago. On the surface, at least, both the nation and the colleges were "fixed" enough in their position so that one need not go to any great lengths in establishing it. The very opposite is true today, however, not only for the colleges and universities but for the federal government's interest in them.

6

The National Setting

What makes our position at the moment so unusual—so rapid in its changes, and so disturbing in its future? I shall deal with this question at the moment primarily from the perspective of the colleges and universities, while I shall naturally imply in my answer many of the forces that underlie our national life. We are in a period of great change and stress for higher education only because our whole society is in that same state.

OUR PRESENT SITUATION

Like every other country involved in the Second World War, we have come to a critical point in our recovery. On the one hand, our economy has nearly stabilized, despite the rough treatment given it. On the other, a generation that knew the war only as a child's dream has begun to move into maturity. Along with it a radical increase of population has begun everywhere in the world to pose ruthless questions. At this precise moment, stability in some quarters is balanced by astonishing shift and change in others. We are not yet at the point where we must battle desperately even to keep ourselves in touch with our immediate educational responsibilities; we still have time to develop some coherent view of what higher education should do for the country, and how it can best accomplish its ends. Within a very few years, however, the pressures upon calm insight will be nearly intolerable; the demands for student spaces, additional faculty, proper plant will leave us no time to look beyond our immediate obligations. It is not too strong to say that unless we define our purposes with complete clarity now, we shall find ourselves hopelessly and dangerously confused by 1970.

THE PURPOSE OF HIGHER EDUCATION

As a result of our critical situation, this book, which in its central portions is devoted to one kind of relationship—that between the federal government and higher education—has also a legitimate interest in the ends of higher education itself. I see these ends from two points of view: first, the areas of understanding, analysis, and insight, with which higher education should be concerned; and second, the national and professional attitudes toward its formal obligations which are most fruitful and most valid. Such a return to our basic purposes is relevant because we have shown such astonishing power at times to bury our real obligations

7

under a landslide of trivia. Whatever we expect to accomplish in the next ten years, we can be sure that we shall get nowhere unless we establish our central obligations and abide by them.

The areas of understanding which most deeply concern us are four in number, and they have this in common: each seeks to "place" human beings, to give each individual some real guidance about who he is, where he is, and what use he may make of his powers after discovering them. One can picture the major disciplines and fields of university education as a spectrum, running from man's inner and most directly personal experience, through his social understanding of every kind, to his evocations of the natural and physical world, and finally to the analytic and abstract constructs by which he creates from his experience patterns of order not directly observable in any part of it. Since they are a spectrum rather than separate kinds of study, any two or more of these fields may combine. In fact, one evidence of the intellectual life at its best is precisely their combination. In minds as different as those of Plato, Dante, and Whitehead we can see the wise interaction of mathematics, history, and symbol, to form some coherent view of man's nature and purpose. The great fields of study will vary from time to time, but the purpose behind them is surprisingly persistent; without it the college or university has no real significance.

DIFFICULTIES IN OUR WAY

The overpowering developments of knowledge in the last 150 years have at times obscured this true and stable purpose of higher education. With no criticism of our own history, we can recognize that the very rapidity with which we have developed has tended to make our colleges and universities more active in the secondary than the final ends of education. Yet at the same time we have reacted with great vigor against our own difficulty; no other country in the world has gone so far in encouraging higher education without professional bias. We have not always been clear about the meaning of our so-called liberal studies; but we take them far more seriously than the casual observer of American society would imagine.

The attitude which tends constantly to obscure the heart of our best education is not one of early professionalism; it is a native compulsion to be sure that we use what we get in school or college. Use is an instinctive standard of value for us. When we have falsely modified a discipline or a department, it is usually in order to prove the immediate utility of what we do. In this way we have often created a clash between utility and enduring value; and the college or university then comes off rather badly as the guardian and revealer of kinds of knowledge which are too rich in meaning to be available for any one immediate purpose.

At this point in time, furthermore, we need the basic and persistent strength of higher education far more than in times of slighter stress and less climactic change. We face here one of many paradoxes in our situation; the very urgencies which push education toward piecemeal tasks are in fact only to be met by a stronger and more coherent idea of higher education than we have had until now. If education is most truly the enterprise which helps man to find himself in his many settings, then we need this kind of education most when the pressures of change and crisis are at us most strongly. In short, at a time when it will be most tempting to make colleges and universities merely useful, we must make sure that they are influential instead.

Education at Its Best

ESSENTIAL ATTITUDES

Perhaps our basic concept of higher education will be clearer if we ask, not only what tasks it is to assume, but what attitudes it should adopt in doing its work. It will help us little if we ask colleges and universities to face the great questions of human purpose, order, and means unless they bring to their work a stature equal to the problems. This can happen only if we define and accept certain central kinds of tone and temper in everything we attempt within higher education in the next ten or twenty years.

These attitudes can be seen in their negatives, first of all; they must be opposed to the routine, the pedantic, the dogmatic and the arrogant. The constant danger of all institutions that pursue "truth," after all, is their urge to claim that they have found it and need look no further. We must now define for ourselves, in our own protection, the positive attitudes upon which higher education must rely if it is to transcend its common limits. We must proceed on the often-voiced assumption that our time demands educational greatness of us; and as a result we had better ask what that greatness is to be. Certainly without some knowledge of it we cannot begin to describe our national obligation.

The first attitude which we must demand of ourselves during the development of college and university life in the next ten years is one of vital and active coherence. This may sound as redundant as asking a centipede to walk; but I doubt that coherence any longer comes easily to the world of higher education. It is not just that we are dealing with great numbers, and shall deal with greater; it is not just that we are dealing with a staggering increase of knowledge, which we can expect to grow as geometrically as the population; it is not just that our campuses are turning into cities, and that our budgets begin to seem more comfortable for corporations than for colleges. All of these things are crucial, immediate and confusing; but all reflect a far more basic fact about our society as it has emerged in the last 300 years. Without any romanticizing of the period prior to the seventeenth century, we can see that many of its interests, convictions, and tendencies were directed toward one center of religious and philosophic conviction. Against the stress and thrust of the renaissance that center could not hold. We cannot wish it back again, but we are at a point, I think, where we must make a serious reckoning with our own centrifugal quality, not asking like romantic medievalists how to dismiss it but learning how to control it in the interest of some reasonable sense of community.

THE CONCEPT OF A FRONTIER

We have one such means of control traditionally available to us in our own society: our sense of frontier, which concerns itself not merely with the physical but with that living and developing edge between the traditional and the new, the discovered and the possible, the established and the incoherent. To have a sense of frontier is, in this way, not the opposite but the obverse of having a sense of history. One begins, at least, to find through it some means of relating present and future as the sense of history relates present and past. The sense of frontier, properly accepted, allows a society to attack with some confidence the problems, not only of its present condition, but of its "becoming," its hidden but insistent future.

At present in western society, this concept of a frontier is particularly important. The greatest demands upon us in the next 20 years will be those of creating relationships where none have existed: between countries whose circle of influence used to be tangential and is now almost concentric; between scientific concepts which used to belong to separate fields and are now simply different ways of looking at the same event; between political theories which used to conflict and now complement; between concepts of artistic style which used to suggest a town or a region, and now reflect a continent or a culture. In each of these cases, we can recognize that the past of a given relationship is far less critical than its future; we can recognize that the attitude of frontier exploration which allows us to make sense of our world now is about to have even greater demands made upon it.

If M. Denis de Rougemont is correct in his analysis of development in Europe and America, we have faced this same problem over and over again. The growth of western society has resulted from the acceptance of a series of frontiers, a sequence of steadily more difficult ways of developing order from the complex, immediate demands of a particular time and a particular society. As many see it, we are at a point where we must go through the same thing again in an even more complex way; and the only alternate to success at defining and mastering our frontiers will be a collapse into hopeless barbarism.

This attempt stands no real chance of success without the college and university. Our world at large is concerned with production, distribution, marketing, services—all the things that keep a complex society (or group of societies) physically alive. Beyond and beneath these necessary activities stand the great questions of purpose, order, and direction which justify our physical and financial actions. Clearly colleges and universities are not the only places where we create a corporate sense of value; and just as clearly they do an inadequate job of it at times. But in a society like ours which often fosters destructive tensions between the traditional and the new in its plans and actions, the university has a unique place. Its constant obligation is to this dual quality in the world of learning: the interpretation of the past, and the exploration of the future. The university in this way bears witness to the continuity of intellectual life, a witness essential for a society whose forms and shapes so often seem to run counter to any real continuity. The university is living and lively proof that an adequate frontier is never merely an isolated new event, but the new as it grows from the established, the understood, the accepted. In this way the new idea takes on meaning; it is new not through its isolation from other ideas but through its relationship to them.

THE PLACE OF THE UNIVERSITIES

The briefest reminder of a few of the recent and legitimate fields of university effort will show, perhaps, how the universities are making their contribution to new senses of national frontier, new insights which imply new obligations. During the last thirty years there has been a striking growth in the sciences which work between and beyond traditional disciplines—biochemistry, geophysics, biophysics and the like. Meanwhile, a similar development has taken place in the sciences of society, with the emergence of integrative disciplines like anthropology, and the extensive use of mathematical means of analysis. In the humanities, we are beginning to move into the serious study, even at the undergraduate level, of non-European societies, literatures, ways of thought that only a short generation ago were taken as esoteric amusements for a few but certainly not as serious preoccupations for the "ordinary" student.

Two things should be clearly understood about this nourishment of the sense of frontier by our colleges and universities. First, it often reflects the half-spoken and still unformulated concern of our whole society about some basic issue. As our world begins to dazzle and confuse us with its many-sidedness, we strike back through the best work of the universities. If we hunger for a new idea to make sense of a new world, that hunger is translated with surprising speed into the formal order of university life.

At the same time this response of the university world to the great and urgent needs of its time is much more than a mere response—at least, it is so when the learned world is truly alive and truly free to live up to its own best possibilities. In that vigorous state, colleges and universities move constantly to tell their society about itself; they cut constantly through the unexamined life, the abortive opinion, the blind prejudice. They make the condition of frontier thinking possible for their world; not only are they the wise servants of their society, but in this respect they are its advisors as well.

Perhaps I had better say that they should be. One of the most urgent problems of the next ten years will be precisely the maintenance in higher education of the resources and the energy to perform this great and even ultimate service for our society. It is easy for us to find jobs for our colleges and universities, but by no means so easy to remember that beyond all the specific tasks there are two or three great enterprises upon which our future depends. National policy for higher education will mean very little, no matter how much it costs, unless we understand clearly that our colleges and universities speak not only for us but to us. We go to them for help, for training, for information; we must also see that they are strong enough so that we can go to them for wise counsel.

This aspect of higher education needs to be understood at the start of our discussion, because it is the easiest thing to lose in a time of alarums and excursions. We will find it far easier in the next few years to build a better guidance system for our missiles than to build a wiser policy for their use. And if the world of higher education has a great responsibility for the first, it has a primary obligation to the second. Any significant planning for our future must recognize the difference between the urgent and the essential. Our national policy for survival must also be broad enough to include in its definitions the survival of the good, the wise, and the humane as well as the clever and the effective.

And this, perhaps, is the real meaning of the frontier as I have described it; it is above all the constantly "new" and yet enduring expression of the best that we know, and the best that we are. It is in this sense that the idea of frontiers stands at the heart of both our national life and our policy for higher education.

The Idea of Excellence

ITS PURSUIT

One of the most literate and forceful expressions of central duty in our national life was the extended discussion of the idea of excellence in the Rockefeller Brothers Fund Report of 1958, *The Pursuit of Excellence: Education and the Future of America.* For a whole host of reasons the phrases of this title speak to our discontent. We have learned in these last years to be profoundly critical of our own unanalyzed but powerful standards: our assumption that size is likely to equal value, our belief that democracy is best expressed in a common level of achievement, our fear of the superior and our worship of the successful. The agonies of conscience which have recently afflicted us have had this virtue at least: they have led us to question seriously whether an unthinking mediocrity was enough to expect of ourselves. Out of this doubt—this critical and maturing doubt—has come our frank and public preoccupation with the idea of excellence.

Now that we have found this new awareness, however, there is some danger that in our characteristic fashion we will pin too much hope on the words, as though they had in them a magic to cure our social and educational ills. "The pursuit of excellence," we say. Like Edna St. Vincent Millay's candle burning at both ends, the phrase gives a lovely light. But what does it mean? It is possible to come to the uncomfortable conclusion that, like the two-ended candle, the pursuit of excellence is not only a single proposition but a precarious one.

This might seem a heretical statement just now, when so many of us are deeply worried about the need for some sort of pervasive excellence to oppose the gaudy and expensive mediocrities of American life. I happen to believe fervently that some such rediscovery of quality is essential; but I have come to have some curious feelings about this matter of pursuing excellence—which sometimes looks a little like a cat chasing its tail.

The image is not a frivolous one. If you consider the words *excellence* and *pursuit,* you will see that they belong together as the tail belongs to the cat. To excel, after all, is to go beyond, to thrust ourselves forth from where we are. But crucial questions remain; do we "go beyond" in this sense merely to project ourselves into the void? Are we concerned to go beyond others, much as in the novel Sammy runs perpetually until he drops; or do we mean to go beyond ourselves so that we gain rather than lose, so that we reach our frontiers as discoverers rather than fugitives? Until we begin to answer questions like these, the pursuit of excellence is nothing but a chase; *excellence* left undefined is as much a word of action as *pursuit*. It is not a goal; it is merely (and at best) a means. It is not a word of substance, but a word of process. And important as the processes of life are, they mean nothing without the ends of life, the ends which (if they are valid) can never be reached, but can define and make firm some substance for words like *excellence, quality,* or *achievement.*

THE NORMS OF SUCCESS

A major aspect of our unspoken faith in our own time and our own society is the conviction that true zeal to excel means progress beyond oneself. The concept lies deeply in our Puritan inheritance, and it received brilliant confirmation from men as different as Jefferson and Franklin—Jefferson with his profound faith in the responsible individual, Franklin with his lively devotion to the pragmatic, constantly inquiring mind. But this concept of excellence as individual growth has been heavily overlaid in the last hundred years by a concept of excellence as competition—and the acquisition of some hard outward signs of successful competition. As we have become progressively less sure during this century about the inner standards we could use in judging our growth and development, so we have become more and more eager for the outer signs by which we could at least prove our competitive victories. We are no longer sure what a good man is, but we have reached some agreement about the trade-mark of a successful one.

And yet we are not at ease about a clash between the good and the successful. Indeed it is this conflict which lends so much weight to our concern today for the pursuit of excellence. Granting that excellence is an operative but valuing word, we in the colleges and universities want to operate well and vigorously. We want the credit of excellence, but we too are victims of clashing definitions. We are often, in fact, as unsure as Socrates' Meno about what we mean by the good; and I suspect that often we are just as eager as Grosse Point or Scarsdale to base our definition on externals. If a noble percentage of our students are at the top of their high school classes, if a great number of them go on to the best graduate schools, if our buildings are bigger and our football teams better, then we assure ourselves that we are concerned about excellence—and furthermore, that we have proved the effectiveness of our concern. We have pursued excellence, and we have finally caught the beast. During these past years, then, we have been the uncritical partners in our society's shift of awareness about excellence. We have accepted without serious question the proposition that real achievement is a matter of outward result.

We like to think that we have something to do with setting standards and goals for our society (and as I have already suggested, it is one of the permanent obligations of a university); it is doubly ironic, then, that in our estimate of ourselves, the standard of excellence has been set for us, and all too often uncritically accepted by us. As a result, we have at times lost track of the possibility that we were denying excellence by the very ways in which we claimed to pursue it. In short we like to prove that we can succeed, but perhaps we, like the rest of our society, hate to go through the private purgatory of learning what it means to excel.

As a result there is a quality both urgent and profound in the problem of defining excellence. If the cult of success is not the right setting for it, what should be the antecedents, the assumptions, the context which give it meaning? Furthermore, once we have asked that question, which involves certain of the basic values and assumptions of democracy, we must move on to a second question: what is the real obligation of education to pioneer in the fields of value and action? What must we do, and not do, if we are to turn *excellence* from an operating or decorative term to a way of life for American education—which will mean, in turn, a way of life for the country?

I have already suggested that the problem of defining excellence is in part a function of the clash between inner and outer concepts of success in American life. It is also a function of the basic issue of democratic relationships, and how we are to define them. Can we in fact define them at all, except by negatives? Is it wiser (or at least safer) to leave all the defining to social externals, to those things which can easily be bought for our adornment? Then each of us could have his private preserve, his inner sense of equality with every other citizen. Shall we simply accept the fact that our own world no longer allows a straightforward Jeffersonian view of our way of life; or shall we go one step further, and recognize that Jefferson's vision never existed except as a vision?

These are major points of definition for our own time. We have inherited from the late nineteenth century a sense of guilt because we promised so much equality of chance in our society and gave so much inequality of life. As a result we would now solve our problems by obliterating differences among men, if we could. The signs of our embarrassment are everywhere: when Ivy League clothes replace the two-pants suit, when the hoodlum, the brilliant entertainer and the international socialite are part of the same set, when every man's education, and his hat, must be like his neighbor's, then we are facing something more serious than casual or good-natured conformity. We are facing the most critical question we can ask about democracy: can it be free enough, can it be true enough to its own ideals to accept the tremendous variety of human desire, awareness, and talent without wrenching that variety toward some easy and common standard?

CONFORMITY AND DIVERSITY

At the same time that we feel eager for certain outward conformities, which will demonstrate our community without our having to work very hard for it, we have tried to eliminate the wearing inner problem of diversity in idea and conviction. One great paradox of democracy has been that it clamors so loudly for the theory of freedom and at times criticizes so caustically the practice of it.

A simple example will suggest how deep the difficulty runs. We recently had a distinguished candidate for the Presidency as one of our College guests. He spoke (or rather, answered detailed questions) about America's relationship to the emerging world community. One of our most able former trustees returned a ticket to the event, saying only that the gentleman in question was definitely "not his boy," and that he didn't care to come. This particular trustee is a person of integrity and intellectual achievement, but when he confronted a man he didn't agree with politically he couldn't exercise his freedom except by staying away. He did not feel, evidently, that in prejudging the case he was calling the heart of democracy into question, but it seems to me that this is precisely what happened. And to add the final ironic fillip, the exchange did not involve a hidebound conservative refusing to listen to a supposedly dangerous liberal, but the precise opposite. A fine and "constructive" liberal felt certain that he already knew enough—perhaps too much—about the other side of the street.

Rejections of this sort at times make our way of life faltering, and inconsistent within itself. A democratic society at its best implies a profound individual responsibility not only for understanding one's world but for acting on the understanding. Only as we develop and guarantee this kind of active insight have we begun to make use of a democratic way of life; and every failure to use it is a failure of democracy—whether we ignore the provocative speaker, reject the difficult painter, or deny the new idea. Democracy is not just a matter of equal rights for all; it is far more basically a matter of the individual and collective *use* of equal rights. Without use they wither, and we may not even notice the death of the inheritance which is also our future.

We must, then, resolve our conflicting assumptions about the opposition of conformity and variety on the one hand, regulation and "freedom" on the other. We must recognize how dangerous our muddy metaphysics are for education in particular; and we must learn to live comfortably and clear-headedly with the kind of paradox from which we draw much of our political strength. For education the paradox might be put this way: a truly democratic policy for education cannot long survive conditions of mere uniformity, mere mass, mere common denominator. The first and most crucial antecedent for any positive result (let alone for excellence) is a recognition of unity in difference—a conviction that we exist as a society to make creative order from our infinite human diversity. One can easily identify societies which do not work this way, but we put our faith in the kind of order which might be described as "variety in action." It is the order called forth by E. B. White's vision of the American college:

> A campus is unique. It is above and beyond government. It
> is on the highest plane of life. Those who live there know the
> smell of good air, and they always take pains to spell truth with
> a small "t." This is its secret strength and its contribution to
> the web of freedom; this is why the reading room of the college
> library is the very temple of democracy.

If we are to give the twin ideas of democracy and excellence any stability for the years just ahead, it must be precisely through our acceptance of the inquiring mind as opposed to the self-centered, the free mind as opposed to the doctrinaire, the committed mind as opposed to the dogmatic. And if we can agree about this, if we prove through our agreement that the vision of responsible democracy is still alive for our time, I believe that we can derive from it and relate to it the great educational needs, goals, and ambitions of the next twenty years. They stand beyond excellence, in a sense, since they are the things in which we wish to excel; but they define excellence, since they and they alone can make it a word of real substance. We should recognize as we speak of them that these are more than goals for education; they are goals for our national life. Formal higher education at its best would be merely one expression of them, one way of bringing them to pass.

Confusion and Clarity in Higher Education

THE NATURE OF OUR DIFFICULTY

Like every other major aspect of our culture, education and the planning for education must cope with the forces of hectic growth and confused change so characteristic of us as a nation. Four aspects of that growth are dominant in our time: the shift from the town to the city, and now to the urban belt or city cluster; the shift from native skill and talent to the highly developed training and education of the individual, which is in turn the reflection of a steadily more complex and specialized society; the shift from a self-contained economy to a world-related one, with all its enormous scope and precarious balance; the shift from a frugal and self-sustained culture to one which, I am tempted to say, possesses affluence without influence—a society of high prosperity and low responsibility.

It is easy enough to see why four such centers of change have created for us and in us a major confusion of goals, standards and powers. Our assumptions about value have traditionally been based on the individual conscience, the small social unit, the frontier of opportunity and escape. Each of these hallmarks of our national character has been changed beyond recognition; and yet until recently we have tried in an uncritical way to maintain the assumptions and the attitudes of that vanished world. We are annoyed, even outraged by our personal and social confusions, but we have not known quite how to move beyond them.

Two or three recent and glaring examples of our confusion may clarify its nature. The tragic events which climaxed the television quiz show hearings remind us almost beyond endurance of our common folly and, actually, of our common guilt. We indicted others for corrupting a particular kind of entertainment; but we should indict ourselves for ever giving it support in the first place. Millions of us seemed to feel that the drama of the intellectual life could be caught up in a series of disparate and unrelated questions. The most brilliantly academic of us were no more exempt from this folly than the tavern keeper or the gas station attendant.

But we have been just as confused in other areas. The recent fiscal arguments in states like Michigan and Wisconsin suggest that all of us know something at first hand about confusion and bafflement of purpose. The monumental struggle of management and labor (whose recent focus was the steel strike) suggests that the country holds at the heart of its economic life a good deal of bewilderment about the purposes appropriate to a free society. Are we free to thwart the common good, or (assuming that we know what the common good is) are we only free to advance it? Are we free to play politics with the financial structure of a great state, or are we only free to give public life our devoted and selfless service? Are we free to play games with our public and private morality, or are we only free to seek our pleasures and our rewards in the context of a society which still, despite its size, stands or falls by the actions of each of us?

As anyone can see, these questions suggest an answer, and an answer which has the profoundest meaning for higher education. Freedom of any kind, in any arena, is a precarious privilege, not an automatic condition of life. If it is not expressed by wise decision and courageous action, it will diminish, and the effectiveness of every major institution in our society will diminish along with it. In higher education we already know how damaging a lack of clear decision on our part can be. Every program undertaken for the wrong reasons, every college kept alive beyond its usefulness, every student cluttering the classroom when his heart and mind are elsewhere—in these and a thousand other ways, higher education is weakened at its heart. Our power to define worthy goals and pursue them is hampered, sometimes almost to the point of paralysis, by these confusions of judgment and action. We cannot hope to reach for excellence until we are willing, not only to define our best purposes but to fight for them.

THE PURPOSES OF FREEDOM

When I say that we must define our purposes, however, I am not suggesting that we engage in another round of institutional self-studies. These have an air of Narcissus about them, and they result all too often in an academic rephrasing of the boy scout laws. What we need to reckon with again are the *final* purposes of American education—the expectation of ourselves which is adequate not only for the urgencies of the moment but for the needs of the century. All of us know too well what the immediate urgencies are: drastic increases of enrollment, budgets which cannot keep pace with necessity, courses of study which shift and change before we have time to learn what they are really about. It is not enough to meet these questions, however. We must use these problems of the moment instead of being used by them, and we must use them in the service of far more complex questions.

First, what is the liberal and nonspecialized education proper for a country that aspires to world leadership without world domination? What must we know of man, of the universe, of technical implement, of clashing national interest, if we are to keep any ideal image of ourselves alive?

Second, what is a college or a university obligated to? Must it confront all the possible fields of study, and all the students who think they want to enter them?

Third, what is the best mode of interaction between scholarship and teaching? Our academic inheritance has shown us the extremes of practice; now what balance of relationship will make for the truest increase of the intellectual life?

Fourth, what public and national expectation of academic life do we want to encourage? (We have never had so good a chance to establish our own image; our very crises bring that opportunity, if we are bold enough to insist on it. And if we do *not* insist on it, we shall become merely the servants of anyone who can pay for a job of training or research. The center of initiative will pass from us; and then we shall not even have the chance to talk about excellence, much less pursue it.)

Coherent decision about these four questions will give us in turn an answer to many of our specific and immediate problems. But it will do far more important things. It will allow us to influence our society rather than merely reflect it; it will allow us to establish our relationship to the permanent frontiers of thought and action. We can then talk about excellence with a clear mind, since we shall have established those things at which we wish to excel. If we agree, for instance, that a man is not truly educated in our time who knows his European past but not his Asian present, then we have begun to suggest a new standard for judging liberal education. If we agree that not all colleges and universities have identical ends, then we shall be free from much of the foolish duplication that wastes our educational resources, and we can pursue excellence in some things rather than sauntering after mediocrity in everything. If we can give public recognition to the fact that the best teaching and the best research are inseparable, we shall then be able to recognize excellence in the intellectual life as something which involves both creative insight and the power to make it understood. Each of these decisions will free us for the pursuit of a certain kind of excellence, and each will play its part in preparing us for that fourth and most pervasive problem, the public understanding of academic value, the point at which beyond all others we must establish a basis for judging quality and achievement.

An adequate answer to our four questions will give us a further result, one which follows directly from those I have already suggested. If we define our purposes clearly enough so that we retain and enhance our initiative, and if we make ourselves free to pursue excellence through the toughness of those basic definitions, then we can talk about federal policy with some hope of real success. The proposition is simple, though with some complex implications. If we know what we want, we can achieve it nationally. If we do not really know, then our most strenuous efforts are likely merely to make our situation more difficult, because they will lead us further into the wrong kinds of enterprise.

Problems of Policy

OUR EDUCATIONAL PURPOSE

Just as we must make up our minds, then, about the kind of democracy we intend to espouse, so we must make our decisions in some detail about educational policy. Perhaps it is important at this point to recognize the order in which these basic decisions ought to be made. We cannot wisely start from a financial base, to which we tailor our ideas. Instead we must start from a base of judgment, from which we can move to some specific estimates of what we need in both men and money if we are to do the essential jobs.

As we define these central jobs, we need above all to understand their unity within the many-sidedness of higher education. The latter is obvious enough if we look around, and see everything from a proprietary school of commerce to a graduate school of oriental languages. But that recognition of our diversity leaves out the crucial fact that so far as the many elements of higher education have meaning, they have it for one another and for our whole society. The individual schools and students involved often fail to recognize the fact; each is busy with his own enterprise, his own individual "vocation." But behind them and within them, so far as they deserve to exist, stands the corporate purpose of a society which, as I described it a few pages ago, has taken on itself the responsibility of leadership without domination.

This kind of leadership is singularly difficult to exercise. It is open to constant perversion and misinterpretation. At this moment, further-more, there is not the slightest guarantee that we shall succeed, since to do so we must compete with some alien and powerful ideas of national purpose. Our position has these major virtues, however: it reflects the best of our own tradition, and if we develop it correctly it has greater relevance to the state of the world than any other conceivable view which a great power might adopt. The greatest need of a hundred emerging countries is for material help, but beyond that they need time and encouragement. (One of the great menaces of the moment, in fact, is the desire of so many new or struggling nations to reach full political sophistication and effectiveness tomorrow, if not today.) A major element in our world responsibility at the moment grows from the fact that we are trying to deal honestly with these new nations. To a greater extent than our critics will allow, our policy toward them is based upon restraint of our own power, our knowledge of the actual needs of others, as opposed to the immediate propaganda advantage which we might gain from pretending to meet their needs. We have been willing, as a result, to face and accept attitudes of great complexity in the building of American policy. Our naiveté in the application of that policy has sometimes been woeful and totally unnecessary; but often it has been the consequence of difficulties which are inseparable from a policy of "controlled power."

I have explored the implications of this policy, because it has great determining significance for American colleges and universities. It is a policy not only for external relationships but for internal as well, not merely for public and governmental actions but for industrial and private ones. It is the mode in which we think, when we are at our best, and it calls for uses of the mind which are almost defining characteristics of both national policy and the educated life. If the discipline of power and the pursuit of complex truth are as essential for the country's welfare as I have suggested, then the question of national policy for education can be rephrased in its proper form as policy in education for the national good. The change in verbal order represents the true state of things—or at least the desired state of things. And it suggests that we can best establish a few national goals for higher education by looking sharply at four or five of the decisions about educational value that concern us most deeply at present. If national policy at its heart is a matter of attitude and spirit rather than of dollars and weapons, then the aspects of higher education which we must protect and develop most vigorously in the years ahead are also likely to be matters of attitude. It is only from our basic assumptions, after all, that any hope of wise planning can come.

FOUR MAJOR ASSUMPTIONS

These assumptions about higher education group themselves around four chief centers: *first,* legitimate fields of study and research, and sensible attitudes toward them; *second,* the relationships within education, between the high schools and colleges on the one hand, the colleges and professional schools on the other; *third,* the nature of the teacher-scholar; and *fourth,* the student himself, in his various roles as instrument, object, victim or even at times center of the academic enterprise. Most major questions of college or university purpose will develop logically from one of these four centers. It may even be that most questions of national or federal purpose in higher education will develop from them as well.

The first center of attitude, which involves the issue of legitimate fields of university teaching and research, is particularly alive and urgent. Not only are we faced with the constant shift and change of knowledge already described, but we feel great competitive pressures urging us to make the most of each new field of technical, productive or even decorative competence. Universities grown great in the service of their regions find it difficult to deny that service now, even though the sheer multiplicity of it tends to obscure or obliterate their real obligations. Colleges which have had trouble staying alive find it hard to resist adding the clever program, the popular but momentary course, the hopeful magnet rather than the better mousetrap. Institutions which have had trouble enough giving an adequate Bachelor's degree now insist on granting the M.A. and yearn toward the Ph.D. We find ourselves in some way confused and compromised; we are pulled constantly beyond wise growth into disorder, into situations where we can no longer be sure of our purposes, let alone whether we are fulfilling them.

Clearly it would be naive to deny the complexity of the modern college and university; we cannot wish away our world. The real question for us, however, is whether we shall reflect our world at its most hasty and unordered, or whether we can to some extent make order and selection from among the host of things that clamor to be done. This question is not asked out of concern for the comfort of life in colleges or universities. It is asked because too rash a use of higher education for secondary or inessential purposes is the surest way to weaken the nation intellectually.

The old seed corn image is relevant here. We have a finite amount of distinguished talent. If we do not use it to advance our most important (as opposed to our most urgent) concerns, we shall in ten or twenty years have a weak base for operation of the universities and therefore for our national life. Certain major industries have begun to realize this. They are starting to release men from their staffs for university service, and they are giving financial support which makes it possible for the universities to compete for skilled manpower on more equal terms with the rest of society. But we have not yet devised many schemes of protection within the universities themselves. We have no assured way of supporting the best as opposed to the best-sponsored research; and we have no way of being certain that the crucial kinds of teaching receive our most serious attention.

Clearly one cannot be doctrinaire about these problems. We cannot legislate the fields of research concentration that are to be taken most seriously or restrict the original and creative teacher to someone else's idea of excellence. But we can do something to maintain an attitude of largeness, magnanimity and good sense in basic university decisions. Our talk about the various crises in education sometimes hinders us here. It encourages the best-meaning boards of trustees or legislative committees to look for desperate answers; and it encourages faculties, deans, and presidents to accept the practice of the day as though it were wise policy.

THE CHIEF KINDS OF ACTION

The first issue before us, then, is the issue of policy itself as it involves the college's or university's inner nature. What does it exist to do—everything that can remotely be called educational, or only certain things? Who should control it—state budget officers, trustee committees, donors with money at hand and jobs to be done? How should it commit its resources—alone, as though it were the only university in the country, or in cooperation with others through some common understanding and division of the country's total needs? We have the constant responsibility to revisit both our inner purposes on any individual campus and our outer purposes as we meet these national needs. It is still an open question whether we shall analyze our natures and duties casually, piecemeal, as the occasion offers; or whether we shall accept this question of the institution's nature and integrity as one of the most serious issues of national policy to be resolved.

Curiously enough, we may find that the real understanding and resolution of this problem involve a certain relinquishment of our separation from one another. We can see why if we look at our second focus of attitudes and policies: the need to articulate and coordinate the education of many young people from the early years of high school on through college and into graduate and professional school. If we must use resources which, however great, are ultimately limited, then we shall have to be sure—both for our students and ourselves—that we are duplicating nothing and ignoring nothing.

We have begun, of course, to make genuine progress with this articulation in the relationship between secondary school and college. The colleges have begun to yield a little sovereignty, and to admit that with adequate safeguards, work of "college level" can be well performed in secondary schools. The schools have begun to accept the responsibility for demanding advanced and mature work of the best students. Though we are only beginning this kind of cooperation, we can already see that it has brought each kind of institution new strength and purpose. By yielding a little independence at the right place, we have all benefited. (And we might contrast this wise cooperation with the deeply unwise action of a generation ago which saw colleges give up many requirements for admission, with the result that both they and the high schools declined in educational quality.)

I describe in some detail what has begun to take place, simply because this one achievement may dramatize the many kinds of policy for wise cooperation not yet established. The relationship between the best undergraduate education and graduate or professional work is still surprisingly primitive. Students are too often asked to repeat what they have already done. As first-year graduate students they would benefit from the same privileges of advanced standing which we are now beginning to extend to them as freshmen in college.

The real issue behind such possible changes goes beyond questions of efficient use of teaching resources and student time—important as it is to make sure that we are wise about our employment of both. The major policy question is that of how we are to picture education. Is it to be the province of many separate and unrelated types of institution, each setting its own laws and assuming that students never learned much of anything until they came under its benign, particular influence? Or is it to be measured by people rather than places, and accomplishment rather than attendance? Obviously one can go foolishly far with this second view, but I question whether we have yet gone far enough. We need to give ourselves at every point new incentives for imaginative recombinations of existing material. We might jar ourselves loose from some of our comfortable formulae if we saw the real possibility of moving able students quickly beyond their routine work at every level. If we could find ways to cooperate on this venture at the high school, undergraduate, and graduate levels we might find that we had achieved a major creative revolution in American education—and precisely at the time when the strain on human and physical resources makes it essential.

This kind of "positive revolution" will mean little, however, if it is a matter of departmental or deanly policy unbuttressed by faculty approval. In fact, for the hopes of the next few years to become anything more, we must have not only approval (which often tends to be a little spineless) but also a kind of stern enthusiasm for the great central job of the scholar-teacher. It is one of the calamities of hasty change that it tends to urge us toward simple solutions as well as simple formulations of problems. There is, for instance, a good deal of encouragement at the moment of the idea that we must meet the shortage of teachers by dividing their functions. There will be a few queen bee scholars, but the rest will busy themselves with the day's work of teaching, and may solace themselves at night with a little second-hand though learned honey.

To doubt the wisdom of this idea should not encourage us to its opposite—the conviction that there is nothing so good for twentieth century scholars as a nineteenth century graduate education. Between these extremes there ought to be an idea of the scholar-teacher adequate to our time and our needs.

This idea is, happily, persistent in our tradition. It seems to break apart into its elements only in times of confusion or danger—times when it seems impossible to know enough to teach anything with certainty, or times when it is perhaps safe to have private knowledge but certainly not safe to tell others about it. We have seen some recent and serious threats to the scholar-teacher from both these quarters; but perhaps neither threat is as serious as the threat posed by mere expediency. We are in need of many more teachers at the college level than the graduate schools are likely to produce through their present doctoral programs. Wouldn't it be wise to devise a new kind of graduate program, which would lead to a different degree—respectable in its own right, but different from the present Ph.D.?

The major objection to this idea is the damage it would undoubtedly do to the causes of real learning and significant teaching. The teacher who teaches merely what others have found out or thought through will never be a significant teacher. His students will never learn to use their minds unless they see him using his. The scholar, on the other hand, who feels no obligation to aid the growth of other minds has cut himself off from one of his greatest sources of stimulation. Without his students, he may find himself more learned and less significant every day. The learning which lasts must come alive in a community—not only the community of a library, but of living and active people. Otherwise the learned life becomes exclusively the concern of the learned; and this is sure death for it.

In the rush of the next few years it may be fatally easy to overlook this problem; but it is crucial in any sound national policy for higher education. The Ph.D. degree may have to change in many ways; I think that it should. We will force a serious split in college and university life, however, if we try to parallel it with other degrees which will only create grades of academic citizenship. Instead we must remember the necessary end—the production of an adequate number of young scholars who wear all the appropriate guild-symbols of learning but who are also alive to the needs of their national community. They will not, like some of their elders, expect to be rewarded for progress and seniority by the dubious privilege of confronting fewer and fewer students. They will expect the full support and respect of the country, however, and it will be an important element of our policy to see that they get the support they deserve.

These three areas in which our decisions of policy will be so crucial predicate a fourth—the student himself. At times we talk about him as a unit rather than a person; and we feel forced to this discourse when we look ahead to a doubling of enrollment. Perhaps the best corrective would be to ask whether it will do any good to have—in 1970—6,000,000 "units" who have been exposed to nothing but the appropriate number of T.V. screens and examination books. If education is to be significant, we cannot measure it by what a student is exposed to, but only what happens inside him. And because this is so, we must decide how many students we can arrange this "inner encounter" for at the various levels of post-high school work and the various degrees of student competence. We must recognize the value of our mixed system of admission to college, at which we sometimes level so much criticism. We cannot solve our problems responsibly merely by making entrance requirements more difficult. We can, however, go much further with the practice of directing students to this or that kind of institution, always with the proviso that if they do unusually well they can move on to something more demanding and more advanced. We can insist, as a matter of national policy, that the privilege of education *at any level* is an earned right in our society and not an automatic one. We can recognize that the education must fit the man, and that we debase both if we allow the indifferent and uncaring student to meddle with a demanding education. We have by no means found our policy in this area; and a great many of our decisions about other aspects of higher education must depend on it.

EDUCATIONAL DECISION AND FEDERAL POLICY

Decisions of this kind may seem remote from issues of federal program and policy; but I hope that it will be apparent by now how necessary it is for our future that we recognize how inseparable from one another and from our common national welfare the great questions of American educational planning are. The most serious single fault of American educational planning in the last ten years, indeed, may have been its willingness to accept a too narrow or uncritical definition of its own problems. Enrollments, adequate staffs, and adequate physical structure have been discussed with vehemence, but not always with full awareness that a wise decision about any one of them would modify the decisions which would then be possible or feasible for the others. As it is, we have often backed into our decisions; and we can hardly be surprised, as a result, if federal policy is confused. It merely reflects the partial nature of the decisions which those of us in the profession have felt able to make.

If I am at all accurate in this estimate, then the questions raised in this opening chapter are the necessary prelude to any historical and factual description of our pattern of federal support to higher education. Furthermore, we shall hope to develop some suggestions about both the responsibilities which must be met in the support of higher education and the possible place of the federal government in assuming a share of that support.

A final word of guidance: *support* in Chapter 2 will be interpreted primarily in a financial sense; but there is no doubt, as Chapters 3 and 5 will make clear, that physical support implies intellectual and moral support as well. It is even arguable that the most important question we can ask about any federal program is not, "What construction or expansion does it make possible?" but "What idea does it encourage?" At least we should keep that possibility in mind as we move now through the maze—indeed the clutter—of programs in higher education that are currently receiving the support of the federal government.

2.

Federal policies and practices in higher education

◆ CHARLES A.
QUATTLEBAUM

In an atmosphere of urgency created by the propaganda fallout from Russian achievements in the conquest of space, the American people have undertaken a re-evaluation of their educational policies and programs. These include relationships of the federal government to education at all levels.

The significance of the federal role in education has grown immeasurably as education has become increasingly important to our national security and progress—and perhaps even to our survival as a free people.

The size of the educational task of the United States staggers the imagination. Our form of government, the national economy, and the national ideal and philosophy of education demand that every citizen be given the opportunity to attain the highest level of education he can.

29

♦ CHARLES A. QUATTLEBAUM is Principal Specialist in Education on the staff of the Legislative Reference Service, Library of Congress. He serves as consultant to committees and members of Congress on matters of legislative policy affecting education and prepares reports designed to serve as informative bases for legislative decisions. He is author of numerous works on the federal government and education and contributor to many reference works and educational journals.

Education has become more and more important to the discharge of responsibilities placed upon the federal government by the Constitution and by subsequent federal law. The federal interest in education now not only inherently transcends all state lines in the United States but, as is evidenced by existing programs, also extends throughout the world —to Americans living in other lands and to our friends and allies. It has become apparent that the survival of the Free World depends upon its economic, military and total strength gained through the education of all free peoples.

Within the last decade a number of prominent Americans have given outspoken recognition to the growing importance of education to the national welfare—and hence to the federal government. In 1949 President Truman declared that "Education is our first line of defense . . . Education is the most important task before us." In 1956 former Senator William Benton observed that "Russia's classrooms and libraries, her laboratories and teaching methods may threaten us more than her hydrogen bombs."

In April, 1957, President Eisenhower admonished the nation that "Our schools are more important than our Nike batteries, more necessary than our radar warning nets and more powerful even than the energy of the atom." In an address before the American Council on Education six months later, Chancellor Franklin D. Murphy of the University of Kansas pointed out that "the future of the twentieth century lies in the hands of those who have placed education and its Siamese twin—research— in the position of priority."

Within recent years the Congress has evidenced a growing concern with education, particularly in its relationships to the national security. The increased Congressional interest has been shown by the extent of discussion of education in committee hearings and on the floor of the House and Senate; by the quantity of material related to education inserted in the Congressional Record; by the number of educational bills introduced, the number reported out of committees, and the number enacted.

During 1957 and 1958, members of the Eighty-fifth Congress introduced about 1,500 bills affecting education, and the Congress enacted at least eighty laws involving education in some way.

The National Defense Education Act of 1958 is the latest major event in a long history of Congressional and Executive actions establishing a number of federal policies but no comprehensive federal policy in education. Some of these policies, particularly some of those pursued in the early history of the United States, relate to education in general, including higher education. Others have promoted elementary and secondary education in certain fields, indirectly affecting higher education. Still other policies have applied almost exclusively to higher education.

The main purpose here is to summarize the long history of the development of federal policies in or affecting higher education, noting a representative number of the programs and institutions established in the course of this development.

Chronological Summary

The following list of landmarks may guide the reader down the chronological trail of federal policies in or affecting higher education. Each landmark gives the date of origin of a particular policy or program. The list is not inclusive, partly because a complete list would be lengthy and partly because some of the dates of origin have not been determined. Temporary or discontinued policies and activities are marked with asterisks.

1777   Initiation of direct administration of educational programs, with instruction of military personnel, including schooling in mathematics.

1785   Commencement of aid to territories and later to states for education, by endowment of schools with public lands.

1787   Commencement of endowment of public institutions of higher education with public lands.

1800   First Congressional appropriation for books, which became the nucleus of the Library of Congress.

1802   Establishment of the first federal institution of higher education —the Military Academy at West Point.

1804   Start of federal provision for education in the District of Columbia.

1824   Establishment of the first Army special service school—the start of a large system now providing education up to college graduate level.

1845   Establishment of the Naval Academy at Annapolis—the second federal institution of higher education.

1862   The first Morrill Act—initiation of federal policy of aid to states for agricultural and industrial education, through land grants for colleges.

1867   Creation by Congress of a federal "Department of Education"— now the Office of Education, serving education at all levels.

1874   Beginning of federal aid to states for nautical schools, now degree-granting institutions—introduction of the principle of federal-state "matching" of the funds for education.

1879   Establishment of a federal school for engravers—probably the beginning of formal inservice training of federal civilian personnel, now including higher education at many institutions.

1890   The Second Morrill Act—introduction of a policy of federal money grants for college instruction in specified subjects.

1893   Establishment of the Army Medical School.

1901   Establishment of the Army War College.

1915   Establishment of the Coast Guard Academy, as such—now a degree-granting institution.

1917   The Smith-Hughes Act—beginning of federal policy of promoting vocational education below college grade.

1918   Initiation of rehabilitation training for disabled veterans.

1919   Origin of policy of federal surplus property disposal to educational institutions.

1920   Establishment of the Reserve Officers' Training Corps at colleges and universities.

1920   Organization of the Graduate School of the Department of Agriculture.

1920   The Smith-Bankhead Act—initiation of the policy of federal-state cooperation in vocational rehabilitation, including education, for persons disabled in industry.

1925   Establishment of the (contract) NROTC, similar to the Army ROTC.

1933   Establishment of the Federal Emergency Relief Administration, which supported various educational programs.*

1935   Establishment of the National Youth Administration, which gave part-time employment aid to college students.*

1936   Convention for the Promotion of Inter-American Cultural Relations—U. S. entrance into broad-scale international educational exchanges.

1937   Creation of the Civilian Conservation Corps, which provided vocational education.*

1937   National Cancer Institute Act—beginning of policy of granting public health service fellowships.

1939   The Civilian Pilot Training Act—provision for federal cooperation with colleges in civilian pilot training.*

1942   Establishment of the Armed Forces Institute—offering high school and college correspondence courses.

1943   (Approximate) Establishment of the Army Specialized Training Program at colleges and universities.*

1944   Servicemen's Readjustment Act—providing unprecedented educational opportunities for veterans.

1946   The George Barden Act—strengthening federal-state cooperation in vocational education.

1946   Establishment of the "Regular" Naval Reserve Officers' Training Corps—considered by some persons to be a full, federal scholarship program.

1946   Atomic Energy Act—initiation of fellowship offerings by the Atomic Energy Commission.

1948   Smith-Mundt Act—establishing a broad program of international educational exchanges.

1949   Federal Property and Administrative Services Act—establishment of a broad policy governing surplus property disposal for educational, health, and civil defense purposes.

1950   Housing Act—origin of college housing loans program.

1952   Inauguration of the fellowship program of the National Science Foundation.

1954   Establishment of the Air Force Academy.

1956   Organization of the Air Force Institute of Technology as a degree-granting institution.

1958   Educational and cultural exchange agreement between the United States and the Union of Soviet Socialist Republics.

1958   The National Defense Education Act—establishing new federal policies in education at all levels.

Origin of Federal Policy

Probably most adult Americans know that historically and under the Constitution education in the United States has developed mainly as a function of state and local governments and of non-governmental organizations and agencies. It is less known that in its infancy the federal government initiated two educational policies: (1) operating educational programs of its own, and (2) aiding the states and territories in financing and otherwise promoting education. Both policies antedate the Constitution, and have, almost from the beginning, included higher and lower education.

The federal government's own educational pursuits can be traced back to instruction in the military service which as early as 1777 included schooling in mathematics. Federal educational programs now cover practically all subjects, at all levels, carried out throughout the United States and in many other parts of the world. Examples are operation of the service academies at home, and education of dependents of federal personnel abroad.

Federal aid to education for the territories began as early as 1785, and later for the states. An ordinance adopted in that year by the Congress of the Confederation for the disposal of public lands in the Western Territory set aside one section in every township for the endowment of schools within that township. In the Ordinance of 1787, providing for the government of the Northwest Territory, the Congress made the clear declaration of policy that "religion, morality and knowledge being necessary to good government and the happiness of mankind, schools and the means of education shall forever be encouraged."

The policy-making importance of the Ordinance of 1787 was recognized by Daniel Webster:

> I doubt whether one single law or any lawgiver, ancient or modern, has produced effects of more distinct, marked, and lasting character than the Ordinance of 1787. . . . It set forth and declared it to be a high and binding duty of Government to support schools and the means of education.

Constitutional Background

Throughout the colonial period in America, and for some time thereafter, education was almost universally regarded as chiefly a parental and church function. E. P. Cubberley and other historians of American education have drawn attention to the fact that at the time of the framing of the Constitution a nationwide system of public educational institutions was only a distant hope of a few statesmen and reformers. In his *Interpretative History of Education,* J. L. Messenger has pointed out that at that time a proposal for federal or state administration of public education would have immediately led to the question, "Which church shall control it?" Since in America there was no established national church, such a proposal would have raised an unresolvable issue.

Furthermore, some of the men who framed the Constitution were the products of the old aristocratic doctrine of education, considering it to be mainly for the leaders and others who could afford it. Being absorbed with their great task of establishing a stable government for the new states, the framers of the Constitution left to the future the solution of many problems, including that of the administration of education.

Inasmuch as the tenth amendment to the Constitution provided that powers not delegated to the federal government were reserved to the states, public education at all levels, as it slowly developed during the nineteenth century, came generally under their jurisdiction. Thus the United States, instead of developing a national system of education such as exists in a number of other countries, has developed many systems. The concept of state responsibility for public education at all levels has accompanied the growth of publicly controlled, nonsectarian education.

At the same time certain provisions of the Constitution have furnished support for a great variety of federal educational programs. Outstanding among such provisions is the general welfare clause. Exercising its constitutional powers to tax and appropriate for the general welfare, the Congress has from time to time provided for federal contributions to the financing of education, as in the case of the land-grant colleges.

Besides the general welfare clause, among Constitutional provisions which have afforded bases for federal educational programs are those giving the federal government various powers to exercise exclusive jurisdiction over the seat of government of the United States and over certain other areas, and the implied power to govern outlying possessions of the United States. In 1931, the National Advisory Committee on education, appointed by President Herbert Hoover, reported finding in the Constitution a total of fourteen warrants for federal activities in education.

However, in the enabling Acts of Congress providing for the admission of at least ten of the states, exclusive authority over public education was reserved to them. In some other Acts the Congress has prohibited federal control over education in the states. In the National Defense Education Act of 1958 the Congress reaffirmed this principle, declaring that the states and local communities have and must retain control over, and primary responsibility for, public education.

Education for National Defense

The federal government has developed a general policy of large-scale training of manpower for national defense. In carrying this out the government has utilized a number of federal schools and institutions of higher education, and has entered into contractual relations with other public as well as private institutions, particularly colleges and universities. The federal institutions such as the Army, Navy and Air Force Academies have given academic training comparable to that of civilian colleges.

EDUCATIONAL PROGRAMS OF THE ARMY

The need for broad education of officers, especially engineers, led to the establishment of the Military Academy at West Point in 1802.

In a bulletin of the Federal "Bureau of Education," published in

1890, Frank W. Blackmar wrote that the Military Academy was graduating yearly "scores of educated men who find their way into various civil pursuits in times of peace, and, as engineers of roads or mines, as officers, scholars, and statesmen, form a valuable portion of the community."

The Morrill Act of 1862, creating the land-grant colleges, and an Act of September 26, 1888, permitting the detail of Army and Navy officers to existing military institutes, established the policy of providing some military education within civilian institutions. This system became the largest source of reserve-officer supply for the Armed Forces.

The Army Medical School was created in 1893 and the Army War College in 1901.

The First World War led to the federal establishment of the Students Army Training Corps at institutions of higher education. It was disbanded in December, 1918. The National Defense Act of 1916, amended in 1920, founded the Reserve Officers' Training Corps at four-year universities and colleges to "qualify students for positions of leadership in time of national emergency." This was something new in federal activities in education, involving direct contracts and close working relationships with civilian educational institutions.

The World War II Army Specialized Training Program, called "the largest university on the face of the earth," by 1943 was established on more than 300 campuses in the United States. Under this program, thousands of soldiers, many of whom would never have been able to go to college in civilian life, were sent to the best universities in the country. This program ended in 1946, a year that marked the resumption of the ROTC program, which had been suspended in 1943. The year also marked a number of other developments in Army education such as establishment of the Army Information, Strategic Intelligence and Army Security Agency Schools, the Industrial College of the Armed Forces and the National War College—all institutions of higher education.

Operated by the Army under direction of the Joint Chiefs of Staff, the Industrial College of the Armed Forces and the National War College are joint service schools of the highest level. In 1948, the Congress further amended the National Defense Act of 1916 to enable the Army to undertake a more extensive utilization of civilian colleges and universities for advanced academic training of selected personnel. The Army's educational programs have since included use of selected civilian institutions of higher education, on a requirements basis, for duty-time training (mainly at graduate level), and also use of cooperating extension divisions of civilian colleges and universities.

EDUCATIONAL PROGRAMS OF THE NAVY

Throughout its history the Navy has carried out educational activities for both its officers and enlisted personnel. The Naval Academy at Annapolis was founded in 1845. In the 1880's the Navy began providing specialist training, for officers and enlisted men, in shore-based schools. The Naval Reserve Officers' Training Corps was created in 1925. The National Defense Act of that year, which authorized the NROTC, stipulated that it should conform as nearly as possible to the Army ROTC. Following Congressional approval of the "Holloway Plan" in 1946, Naval Reserve Officer Training was expanded to include the "Regular" NROTC, the "Contract" NROTC, and the Naval aviation college program. All of these enrolled college students.

Initiation of the "Regular" or "Holloway Plan" NROTC was a departure from former policy in providing training for reserve officers. The "Regular" NROTC has been regarded by some persons as a full, federally financed undergraduate scholarship program.

During World War II, Dean Joseph W. Barker, Special Assistant to the Secretary of the Navy, said: "The Navy itself has become one huge school. No officer or enlisted man ever ceases going to school in the Navy."

Since World War II the Navy has been adapting its educational plans to rapidly changing needs by increasing emphasis on college graduate courses, especially in engineering, by creating new programs such as the Navy Enlisted Scientific Education Program, and by expanding its instruction to include such advanced studies as nuclear power and guided missiles.

The Navy's "Five-Term College Training Program" (instituted in 1946) has provided education up to baccalaureate level at civilian colleges and universities for certain officers, to permit them to compete for promotion on an equal basis with officers graduated from the Naval Academy or civilian colleges. This training has been wholly subsidized by the Navy. The officer-students have received their ordinary pay and allowances for a maximum of five terms or semesters.

The Navy's graduate training of officers has utilized the U. S. Naval Postgraduate School (awarding advanced academic degrees), the Engineering School, General Line School, Navy Management School, and civilian institutions.

The Navy Enlisted Scientific Education Program has provided a four-year college education, at civilian institutions, for selected enlisted personnel.

The Naval Aviation College Program makes it possible for selected naval aviation candidates to receive two years of college training, and after completion of one tour of sea duty to receive two additional years of training leading to graduation from college.

As a component of the Navy, the Marine Corps has carried out some of its educational programs and has shared in others.

EDUCATIONAL PROGRAMS OF THE AIR FORCE

Under an Act of April 3, 1939, the Army Air Forces received authority to institute their own educational system and began carrying out a large program, which was greatly expanded under the stress of World War II. Lack of classrooms and other facilities led to the leasing of nearly 500 hotels, theaters and other structures for housing and training facilities. The Air Force created an officers' candidate school and an officers' training school, and entered into contract with hundreds of civilian technical schools, colleges and universities for the training of specialists.

On September 18, 1947, the Army Air Forces became the autonomous United States Air Force, which has developed the unique policy, among the military services, of training through a university system (the Air University) as well as through a service academy (the Air Force Academy) and other administrative arrangements. The Air University has included the Air War College, the Air Command and Staff College, the School of Aviation Medicine, the Air Force Institute of Technology, and the Air Force Reserve Officers' Training Corps.

First called the Air School of Application when set up in 1919, the Air Force Institute of Technology has given engineering education to officers for over forty years. It became a degree-granting institution in 1956.

The Air Force Academy, also degree-granting, was established by an Act approved on April 1, 1954. The first class was graduated June 3, 1959.

DEFENSE DEPARTMENT CIVILIAN EDUCATION POLICIES

The Department of Defense affords educational opportunities to civilian employees for two purposes: (1) to give professional workers additional study needed to maintain proficiency in their specialized fields, and (2) to encourage advancement of competent employees by aiding them in education related to their work.

In addition, the military services in 1952 initiated cooperation with the Association of American Medical Colleges, the United States Public

Health Service, and the Federal Civil Defense Administration in a program of "Medical Education for National Defense." The object has been to improve the medical school curriculums in aspects of military medicine and surgery.

Following are a few of the highlights in the development by the military services of the training of civilian employees:

In 1945 the War Department established a school to train persons for staff civilian personnel offices during emergency conditions.

In 1951 the Army began training civilian employees in non-government facilities. This has included academic training primarily in engineering and scientific fields, and special technical seminars at the college level.

Starting with a "management intern" program in 1949, the Navy began steady expansion of its formal developmental programs for selected civilian employees. These have included "on-the-job" training and related academic study at college level.

In 1950 the Navy Department began active cooperation with local colleges and universities in special courses and degree programs of interest to administrative and professional employees of the Department.

On the basis of studies made by industrial personnel experts, in 1951 the Air Force adopted a civilian personnel training policy based upon needs. It has encompassed education at the secondary and higher levels. Under the cooperative education program students have alternated periods of attendance at a participating college with periods of employment at an Air Force installation. Another program has provided selected employees with scientific and technical courses at civilian universities. In 1946 the Air Force began arranging for graduate study by certain employees at colleges and universities located near Air Force bases.

HIGHER EDUCATION IN THE COAST GUARD

In 1876 an Act of Congress provided for the training of officers for the Coast Guard, then called the Revenue Cutter Service. A permanent shore academy was established at New London, Connecticut, in 1910. In 1915 this became the Coast Guard Academy. Graduates, like those of the Military, Naval, and Air Force Academies, receive commissions and academic degrees.

EDUCATION OF CIVILIANS DURING WORLD WAR II

During World War II the federal government carried out or promoted certain educational activities designed to prepare the civilian population for more effective support of the war effort. Some of the older federal educational programs were adapted to wartime needs, and programs representing new federal policies in education were initiated. These included: (1) the apprentice-training service; (2) the training-within-industry service; (3) the National Youth Administration (liquidated as of January 1, 1944); (4) vocational training for war production workers; (5) food production war training; (6) engineering, science and management war training; (7) visual aids service; and (8) the student loan program. Much of the total program, but particularly the engineering, science and management training, was at the level of higher education and involved close working relationships with colleges and universities.

Not only the War Manpower Commission and the Office of Education, but also the Office of Civilian Defense, the Office of Defense Transportation, the Office of Inter-American Affairs and the Office of Lend-Lease Administration carried out or supported some higher-level education related to the war effort.

THE NATIONAL DEFENSE EDUCATION ACT

In passing the National Defense Education Act of 1958 the Congress took its most important policy-making action affecting education in recent years. In the first title of the Act the Congress declared that its purpose was to provide substantial federal assistance in various forms to individuals and to states and their subdivisions, in order to insure trained manpower of sufficient quality and quantity to meet the national defense needs of the United States.

Each of the ten titles of the Act initiated a new federal policy. An example is the federal contribution of (generally) ninety percent of the capital of loan funds at institutions of higher education for low interest loans to students.

Authorizing federal appropriations totaling more than a billion dollars, principally over a period of four years, the National Defense Education Act touches every level of public and private education. Following is a list of its provisions, by title:

I. General provisions—purpose and definition;
II. Loans to students in institutions of higher education;
III. Financial assistance for strengthening science, mathematics and modern foreign language instruction;
IV. National defense fellowships;
V. Guidance, counseling and testing; identification and en-

couragement of able students; counseling and guidance training institutes;

VI. Language development—centers for research and studies; language institutes;

VII. Research and experimentation in more effective utilization of television, radio, motion pictures and related media for educational purposes;

VIII. Area vocational education programs;

IX. Science Information Service;

X. Improvement of statistical services of state educational agencies.

The October-November (1958) issue of *School Life,* published by the Department of Health, Education and Welfare, contains detailed information concerning the provisions of the Act.

Early Federal Grants Policy

In 1802 the Congress of the United States took definite action in continuation of the general support of education initiated seventeen years earlier by the Congress of the Confederation. With the admission of Ohio to the Union in 1802, Congress began designating lands for school support at the time of admission of a state.

Under a provision of the Ordinance of 1787 for a grant of two townships for "a literary institution, to be applied to the intended object by the legislature of the State," a contract was arranged with the Ohio Company which assured to the State of Ohio two townships of land for the support of a university. The land was used to endow the State University at Athens, known as the Ohio University. Other new states also received lands for the endowment of universities. Each State admitted to the Union after 1802, except Maine, Texas, and West Virginia, received two or more townships of land for the purpose of endowing a university. Occasionally since 1803 federal lands have been granted to specifically designated educational institutions. During the first half of the nineteenth century the Congress also made certain monetary grants to states which were used in many cases to support education.

Except for the few grants to specific institutions, the early land and monetary grants were without specification as to the kind of education to receive aid. The Congress pursued a policy of giving financial support to education without attempting to influence the services of the school systems and educational institutions receiving support.

In his history of school finance in the United States, Fletcher Harper Swift has pointed out that the funds created out of the federal land grants were the first stable support for free public education in more than half the states. Undoubtedly the grants strengthened public as related to private education at all levels and set a precedent for other forms of federal aid to education.

Education in Special Federal Jurisdictions

The federal government early assumed responsibility for the education of persons residing in areas under its special jurisdiction. Formerly the largest of these were the territories, where education at all levels was offered. Areas of special federal jurisdiction now include the District of Columbia, reservations such as military posts, Indian reservations and national parks, and the outlying possessions.

In 1804 an Act of Congress approved the administration of education in the District of Columbia by established authorities; subsequent acts delegated the administration to these authorities. The organic act of 1906 for the educational system in the District of Columbia and other legislation has made clear the continuing policy of Congress to maintain in the District a complete system of education as that term is commonly understood in the United States—including higher education, at least to the extent of operation of a teacher-training institution.

Provisions of the Constitution, treaties, legislative acts and court decisions have contributed to the education of Indians living on reservations. The Office of Indian Affairs, which since its creation has administered educational services for Indians, was established in 1824. Lodged in the Department of the Interior since 1849, the Office has provided for the education of Indians through day schools and boarding schools and federal payments to states.

As a responsibility incidental to the building of the Panama Canal, the government in 1905 took steps to establish a system of public education in the Canal Zone. Besides elementary and secondary schools, there is now a junior college.

The varying conditions on federal reservations have led from time to time to different federal provisions for education in these areas. It is noteworthy that the policy has been expressed in recent actions. Acts of Congress within the last decade have established general policies for education on federal properties.

Contracts with Colleges for Research

As early as 1830 the Secretary of the Treasury entered into a contractual arrangement with the Franklin Institute of Philadelphia for an investigation of the causes of explosion of steam boilers. During World War I the federal government began large-scale contractual agreements with colleges and universities for research activities connected with national defense. Some such arrangements were continued after the war. The scope of such research and the number of fields of investigation were greatly increased during World War II.

Within the last several years a considerable portion of the large expenditures for the research programs of the federal government has been going to colleges and universities through grants and contracts. The federal government has developed a broad utilization of the facilities of colleges and universities for research purposes.

There has been much disagreement concerning the extent, if any, to which government research contracts have generally given financial aid to the institutions. Some investigators have said that these "practical" research projects, predominantly in the natural sciences, have created problems for the institutions. Cited problems have included the development of an imbalance between the teaching and research functions, and impairment of the need for the colleges and universities to advance the frontiers of knowledge through theoretical research.

The government contracts have given important, if indirect, financial aid to many students in the form of opportunities for employment in research, often with credit toward advanced degrees. Altogether the contracts have had effects upon higher education so extensive that they must be considered in a following chapter.

Land-Grant Colleges and Associated Services

With the passage of the Morrill Act of 1862 the Congress began giving aid to the states for higher education in certain specified fields. Agricultural and industrial expansion had emphasized the need for more and better education in the natural sciences. The Congress took action to insure the development in each state of at least one college adapted to the needs of agriculture and industry.

THE COLLEGES

The Act provided a grant of federal lands or land scrip to each state in the amount of 30,000 acres for each senator and representative in

Congress from that state. It gave scrip to the states in which there were not sufficient federal lands to make up their allotments. The proceeds of the sales of these grants were to be used for the endowment and support of colleges "to teach such branches of learning as are related to agriculture and the mechanic arts, in such manner as the legislatures of the states may respectively prescribe." The Act also required the teaching of military science.

Congress later enacted the Second Morrill Act (1890) and other loans for continuing annual appropriations to these institutions. They now number 68. Commonly called the land-grant colleges and universities they have also sometimes been referred to as "democracy's colleges," because of the impetus they gave to the expansion of public higher education.

In the second Morrill Act, the Congress introduced the policy of federal money grants for instruction in certain branches of higher education. The Act specified subjects, required annual reports to a federal agency, and provided for withholding of federal funds under certain conditions. It set a pattern for subvention programs not only in education but also in other fields.

The federal grants for these institutions have markedly influenced the course of higher education in the United States, by contributing significantly to its expansion, and by stimulating state support of education in agriculture, engineering and the natural sciences.

THE EXPERIMENT STATIONS AND EXTENSION SERVICE

With the Hatch Act of 1887 the Congress initiated the granting of funds to each land-grant college for the establishment and maintenance of an agricultural experiment station. This was the first Act giving funds to the states for "practical" research. Continuing annual appropriations for this purpose were increased by several subsequent acts. The Department of Agriculture has administered the federal funds for the experiment stations, which have helped provide a scientific basis for agricultural education at all levels.

Through the Smith-Lever Act of 1914, the Congress formulated cooperation with the states in extension work in agriculture and home economics. Pursuant to the intent of Congress, this program has been carried out in connection with the land-grant colleges. Subsequent acts have further developed the basic federal policy and provided additional funds for this work, with the requirement of "matching" by state, college, or local funds for participation in the program. The Secretary of Agriculture has the responsibility for administering the federal funds.

Acts of Congress in 1924 and 1937 authorized certain reforestation activities involving extension work and the land-grant colleges.

In the study of the federal government and higher education made for the Commission on Financing Higher Education, Richard G. Axt named four characteristics of the policy which led to the grants for the land-grant colleges and associated services. In brief these characteristics were:

(1) The federal policy toward higher education was influenced by public land policy and the interests of farmers; (2) it emphasized vocational and professional rather than "liberal" education; (3) it included emphasis on "practical" scientific research; and (4) accented the education of the many rather than a select few.

The Role of the Office of Education

In 1866 the National Association of State and City School Superintendents presented a memorial to Congress urging the creation of a federal educational agency. Subsequently, Representative (later President) James A. Garfield introduced a bill for this purpose. The bill, signed by President Johnson in March, 1867, set up a federal "Department of Education" headed by a Commissioner. Since then, Congressional and Executive actions have several times changed both the name of the agency and its position in the federal structure. As the "Office of Education" it has been a constituent of the Department of Health, Education and Welfare since the creation of that Department in 1953.

The primary function of the Office of Education, as set forth in the establishing act, has been to collect such statistics and facts as shall show the conditions and progress of education, to diffuse information to aid the people of the United States in the establishment and maintenance of efficient school systems, and otherwise to promote the cause of education at all levels. Subsequent acts and Executive orders have added responsibilities for administering federal grants-in-aid to education, cooperative research, special programs and studies, and other functions.

The Office of Education has served as the principal agency of the federal government for formulating educational policies and coordinating elementary, secondary and higher educational activities at the national level. In carrying out its work the Office has cooperated with other government agencies, the states and territories, professional groups and institutions, citizen groups and individuals and international agencies.

ROLE OF THE OFFICE IN HIGHER EDUCATION

The Act establishing the Office of Education required the commissioner to audit the several grants of land made by Congress to promote education, including those for the land-grant colleges under the Morrill Act of 1862.

Pursuant to the second Morrill Act of 1890 and subsequent delegation of authority by the Secretary of the Interior, the Office of Education has since administered federal grants-in-aid for the further endowment and support of the land-grant institutions.

An Act of Congress in 1928 charged the "Bureau of Education" to make an annual inspection of Howard University.

Among the several emergency programs administered by the Office of Education during World War II was the Engineering, Science and Management War Training Program. In cooperation with degree-granting colleges and universities the Office carried this out for the organization of short courses of college grade designed to meet the shortage of engineers, chemists, physicists and production supervisors.

The Office also administered the Student War Loans, which furnished assistance in designated technical and professional fields, and projects for research in universities.

Through the years, the Division of Higher Education in the Office of Education has been assigned, and now carries out, among other duties, the responsibilities for: (1) formulating plans, policies and procedures for higher education; (2) administering funds appropriated for the land-grant colleges and universities; (3) allocating funds for loans to students in higher education; (4) allocating funds for fellowships in graduate schools; (5) negotiating federal contracts for centers for teaching modern foreign languages, for training to improve the qualifications of counseling and guidance personnel, and for the operation of institutes for advanced training in the use of new teaching methods and instructional materials; and (6) advising the Housing and Home Finance Agency on educational eligibility of institutions seeking loans for college housing.

The Division of Higher Education has been carrying out its work through the College and University Administration Branch, the Higher Education Programs Branch, and the Financial Aid Branch.

The College and University Administration Branch—has been promoting improvement in the organization and administration of higher education. It has conducted and published field studies and consulted with representatives of higher education.

The Higher Education Programs Branch—has been promoting improvement in the liberal arts and graduate and professional education, with emphasis on social science, as well as on physical sciences and mathematics, teacher education, and engineering. It has worked through conferences, institutes, publications and addresses.

The Financial Aid Branch—has been responsible for the administration of the National Defense Education Act of 1958 as it pertains to higher education. The Branch has administered the National Defense Student Loan Program, the National Defense Fellowship Program, and the Language Development Program authorized by the Act. The Branch has also been responsible for the establishment of counseling and guidance training institutes authorized by the Act for the identification and encouragement of able students.

Commenting upon the future role of the Office of Education, in October, 1959, the United States Commission of Education said in part:

> The future role of the Office can be readily envisaged as a natural and necessary development of the decades of experience in these areas of activity: (1) statistical and informational services, (2) surveys and consultative services, and (3) participation in financing educational facilities and programs. Judging from the past history of the Office of Education, the increasing national interest in education can continue to be served by assistance without interference and leadership without domination. The Office of Education was instituted as an integral part of the Nation's total educational enterprise, and the significance of Office activities has been enhanced by the deepening realization that education is intimately related to all major fields of national and international concern.

Vocational Education and Rehabilitation

For many decades the federal government has engaged in the carrying out, financing or otherwise promoting vocational programs for civilians, some in higher education.

NAUTICAL EDUCATION—MERCHANT MARINE

An 1874 Act of Congress established nautical schools at six designated ports. This Act inaugurated the principle (already mentioned) of "matching" funds. It provided that a state or locality would receive federal funds equal to the amount appropriated by the state or local government. The training in the nautical schools was later consolidated in four institutions, known as state maritime academies. These train Merchant Marine officers, who upon graduation receive the degree of bachelor of science.

In 1938 the Maritime Commission established the Merchant Marine Cadet Corps, which in 1941 began operating the Merchant Marine Academy at Kings Point, Long Island. This became a permanent, degree-granting institution. Kings Point is to the Merchant Marine as West Point is to the Army and Annapolis to the Navy, except that its graduates become employees of steamship companies rather than of the federal government.

IN-SERVICE TRAINING OF GOVERNMENT PERSONNEL

The federal policy of affording and encouraging in-service training of government personnel appears to have had its origin in the form of an apprentice school for engravers, started by the Bureau of Engraving and Printing in 1879. Thirty years later the National Bureau of Standards instituted technical training for employees, which later led to the organization of the National Bureau of Standards Graduate School. The well-known Graduate School of the Department of Agriculture was organized in 1920, principally for advanced training of federal personnel. Its certificates of credit are accepted by graduate schools of a number of colleges and universities.

An Act of Congress approved July 7, 1958, declares that self-education by federal employees shall be supported and extended by government-sponsored programs.

Systems of in-service training in the federal government now vary widely. They comprise many types of courses and instruction, mainly at the secondary level and above.

VOCATIONAL EDUCATION BELOW COLLEGE GRADE

Federal promotion of vocational education below college grade undoubtedly has had important effects upon higher education. By passing the Smith-Hughes Act of 1917, for example, the Congress created a new federal policy in agricultural and industrial education. This Act extended below college grade a stimulus similar to that given at the higher level through the Morrill Act of 1862.

Acts of Congress in 1929, 1934, and 1936 continuing and extending the promotion of vocational education below college grade were superseded by the George-Barden Act of 1946, which added new services. Further extension was made by the 84th Congress, which legislated training for practical nursing, for the fishing industry, and for teaching vocational subjects. The laws have required dollar-for-dollar matching of federal funds with state or local funds, except for instruction in practical nursing during the years 1957 and 1958.

VOCATIONAL REHABILITATION

In the Smith-Bankhead Act of 1920 the Congress began to provide federal funds for cooperation with the states in the vocational rehabilitation of persons disabled in industry. A number of subsequent acts, including the Social Security Act as amended in 1939, have changed the federal provisions for this program, which utilizes education at all levels. About 20 percent of the total federal funds for vocational rehabilitation is used for education of disabled persons.

AERONAUTICAL EDUCATION

Pursuant to the Civilian Pilot Training Act of 1939 the Civil Aeronautics Administration organized a program of civilian pilot training in cooperation with colleges throughout the country. The program was discontinued five years later.

The Federal Aviation Agency, which succeeded the Civil Aeronautics Administration in January, 1959, currently aids and encourages the development of aviation education by furnishing technical assistance and guidance to schools, colleges and educational bodies.

Education for Veterans

Vocational rehabilitation training for veterans dates from World War I. The Vocational Rehabilitation Act of 1918 provided substantially that any discharged veteran of World War I unable to carry on a gainful occupation should be given such course of rehabilitation as the Federal Board for Vocational Education should furnish. The Act imposed upon the Board the responsibility for facilities, courses and instructors, pay allowances for maintenance and support of trainees, and other things necessary for vocational rehabilitation and placement. Section 3 of the Act provided for training, but not maintenance allowances, for honorably discharged veterans disabled but not seriously handicapped vocationally.

In 1921 Congress established the Veterans Administration and assigned its duties and powers previously exercised by the Federal Board for Vocational Education respecting disabled veterans. Unlike the Federal Board for Vocational Education, the VA did not establish educational institutions of its own although given authority to do so.

The Vocational Rehabilitation Act of 1943, commonly referred to simply as "Public Law 16," afforded vocational rehabilitation training benefits for veterans of World War II like those given disabled veterans of World War I.

The Servicemen's Readjustment Act of 1944 (often referred to simply as Public Law 346) extended education to veterans in unprecedented scope. Most veterans were eligible. Each was free to select his own course of study, his school, college or other training establishment approved by the authorized agency in the state in which the establishment was located. He was allowed time not in excess of one year plus the number of months he was in the service, not in excess of forty-eight.

The law prohibited control or supervision by any federal agency over any state educational agency or any educational or training institution participating in this program.

Except for certain cases under Public Law 346, as amended, both Public Law 16 and Public Law 346 terminated on July 25, 1956. Similar benefits were later extended to veterans of the Korean conflict.

But Public Law 550 modified veterans' educational benefits. Under a simplified system of allowance, the individual veteran became responsible for payments to the educational institution.

In the history of federal policy, the Servicemen's Readjustment Act of 1944 has been called "the twentieth century Morrill Act." It led to enrollment of unprecedented numbers of college students and gave thousands of young people an education they might not have got otherwise.

Surplus Property Disposal

In 1919 Congress passed and the President approved an act authorizing the Secretary of War to sell to educational institutions "at 15 percentum of their cost to trade," World War I surplus machine tools under control of the War Department. Later acts, before World War II, authorized the Armed Forces to donate to educational institutions certain specified surplus equipment needed for vocational educational purposes.

During World War II the government accumulated huge quantities of property which later became surplus, and some of this was made available for education, public health, and civil defense.

SURPLUS PERSONAL PROPERTY

The Surplus Property Act of 1944 provided for transfers of personal property to educational and health institutions at discount from fair value, and for donation of personal property to such institutions when the administrative cost of other disposal would exceed the recoverable value. In 1946 the Office of Education began determining the educational need for such property and its allocation among the states and territories.

In 1948 Congress further developed the policy. It authorized the Armed Forces to donate personal property to schools, colleges and universities upon determination by the Commissioner of Education that such property was needed and usable.

The Federal Property and Administrative Services Act of 1949 repealed some of the earlier legislation and made surplus personal property of all executive agencies available by donation to educational institutions. Amendments in 1950 and 1956 made such property also donable for public health and civil defense.

Under existing legislation, the General Services Administrator is authorized, in his discretion, to give surplus federal property which has been determined to be usable and needed for education, health or civil defense *to established state agencies* for distribution to eligible institutions within the respective states. The Secretary of Health, Education and Welfare is expected to decide what surplus federal property is needed for health, educational and civil defense purposes. (He has delegated the responsibility respecting civil defense to the Director of the Office of Civil and Defense Mobilization.) The Secretary is also responsible for equitable allocations of such property to the state agencies, and for establishing minimum standards of operation. The administration of the Secretary's responsibilities is centralized in the Office of Field Administration of his Department.

REAL PROPERTY

The Federal Property and Administrative Services Act of 1949, as amended, established a federal practice of selling or leasing surplus real property for education or public health where need exists. With respect to determination of selling or leasing price the legislation takes into consideration the benefits that have accrued or will accrue to the United States from such use. The responsibilities of the Administrator of General Services and of the Secretary of Health, Education and Welfare

are essentially the same in the surplus personal property program, already described.

Institutions recipient of federal surplus real property pay for it partly in cash and partly in public benefits accruing through the institutions. Public benefits, which are predetermined by the program use, may justify a full 100 percent discount.

Depression-Period Programs and Policies

During the depression of the 1930's the federal government carried out educational activities as aspects of relief. For example, the Civilian Conservation Corps, created by Congress in 1937, offered vocational training as well as employment to youth in need of jobs. The Federal Emergency Relief Administration, established in 1933, worked widely in the states, giving part-time employment to college students and to out-of-work teachers. The emergency agency, first called the Works Progress Administration, and later the Works Projects Administration, supported a large number of projects ranging from literary classes to college education. The National Youth Administration, established in 1935, gave work training to unemployed youth and part-time jobs to needy college students.

The Public Works Administration made numerous grants and loans to states and municipalities for the construction of school and college buildings. The Reconstruction Finance Corporation also made self-liquidating loans to states, municipal authorities and institutions for educational projects.

Recommendations of Advisory Commissions

An historical review of federal policies in or affecting higher education might well take into account the relevant recommendations made from time to time within the last several decades by important governmental and nongovernmental advisory groups. A number of such groups of prominent laymen and educators convoked by action of the Congress, the President, or heads of federal agencies have made recommendations concerning federal educational policies and programs. National advisory groups affiliated with nongovernmental organizations interested in education have added their voices.

The conclusions of these advisory groups usually have been based upon extensive research and deliberations, often covering a period of years.

Altogether, millions of dollars have been spent within the last few decades to finance the commissions' studies and reports. Some of them have been voluminous, one of the committees alone having published 21 reports and staff studies.

Most of the recommendations of these commissions have been applicable to education in general or to elementary and secondary rather than to higher education. There are notable exceptions. The purpose here is to identify a representative number of the advisory groups and list some of their recommendations.

GOVERNMENTAL ADVISORY COMMISSIONS

In 1931 the National Advisory Committee on Education appointed by President Herbert Hoover drew attention to the extensiveness of federal educational activities and their wide dispersion throughout the federal structure. The Advisory Committee on Education appointed by President Franklin D. Roosevelt, in its report published in 1938, affirmed these findings of the earlier committee. In 1948 the Task Force on Education appointed by the Commission on Organization of the Executive Branch of the Government (the first Hoover Commission) reported that virtually every major department and independent agency of the federal government was participating in educational activities.

With respect to other educational matters the recommendations of these commissions varied. The National Advisory Committee on Education (1931) observed that the federal government had no inclusive and consistent policy as to what it should or should not do in the field of education. The Committee recommended establishment of a comprehensive, forward-looking and coherent federal policy. It also recommended: (1) federal aid to the states for education in general; (2) further development of federal research and informational services; (3) extension of educational activities of the United States in cooperation with other countries; and (4) establishment of a Department of Education with a Secretary in the President's cabinet.

The Advisory Committee on Education (1938) recommended a number of new federal grants-in-aid including aid for improved preparation of teachers and for educational research, planning and demonstration. Among other recommendations of the Committee were those for federal aid to students from 16 to 24 years of age, and establishment of an interdepartmental committee to coordinate the educational activities of the federal government.

The President's Commission on Higher Education, appointed by President Truman in 1946, was composed of representatives of various

fields of public life, including both public and private higher education, and of the three principal religions. The Commission submitted the
six volumes of its report in late 1947 and early 1948. It recommended
expansion of federal activities in higher education, proposing: (1) federal
grants to the states to support a program of undergraduate scholarships
for at least 20 percent of the nation's undergraduate non-veteran students,
and a broad federal graduate fellowship program; (2) a general system
of operating grants to the states for public higher education; and (3)
capital grants to the states for needed buildings and equipment for
public higher education, the federal government to pay one-third of the
total outlay for this purpose.

With respect to the federal grants for current operating expenses,
the Commission recommended that each state's share be determined in
accordance with an objective formula designed to measure the state's
relative need for higher education and its relative ability to finance
an adequate program.

The 1953 Commission on Organization of the Executive Branch of
the Government (the second Hoover Commission, appointed by President
Eisenhower) and its task forces made a number of recommendations
concerning the educational programs of particular federal agencies,
notably several within the Department of Defense. The Commission
also recommended termination of loans for college housing, and greater
federal financial support for basic and medical research.

The report of the Commission on Intergovernmental Relations (established in 1953) confined its concern with education mainly to general
public education and to that at the elementary and secondary level—
the school lunch programs, school construction and operation in certain
federally affected localities, and vocational education. A study committee
report submitted to the Commission also dealt mainly with these matters,
but said that certain principles which it outlined applied to all levels
of education. The committee stated that "whether federal aid should
be extended in the field of higher education involves considerations so
complex that they cannot adequately be disposed of by this Committee
in the time available."

The White House Conference on Education (1955) restricted itself to
consideration of problems affecting elementary and secondary education,
strongly recommending federal aid for this purpose. The President's
Committee for the conference recommended the holding of a White
House Conference on Higher Education. The President's Committee
and several of the preliminary state conferences recommended strengthening the United States Office of Education.

The President's Committee on Education Beyond the High School

(1956) drew attention to the growing proportion of the population seeking education beyond the high school, and to the increasing demands of our economy for men and women with post-high school training. The Committee made about a dozen principal, detailed recommendations concerning the federal government. These included, in brief and in substance, the following: (1) the federal government should avoid policies that threaten control of non-federal educational institutions; (2) the total impact and individual continuing importance of the federal programs affecting higher education should be given thorough study; (3) there should be established a more effective means of reflecting the views of educational institutions and of associations, states, and lay citizens in federal policy determination and program planning for activities relating to post-high school education; and (4) functions of the Office of Education relating to education beyond the high school should be strengthened.

Among other recommendations, the President's Committee on Scientists and Engineers (1958) advocated that the federal government at the White House level should assume responsibility for coordinating and stimulating the nation's efforts in the development of highly trained manpower.

NONGOVERNMENTAL ADVISORY COMMISSIONS

Within recent years various advisory groups affiliated with national, nongovernmental organizations interested in education have published criticisms and recommendations concerning the administration of federal activities in education. Like the governmental commissions already enumerated, these bodies have usually arrived at their conclusions after extensive study and deliberation. Their criticisms and recommendations concerning federal policies in education through the years have related mainly to aid to the states. Even if applied only to the elementary and secondary levels, these recommendations are nevertheless of concern to higher education. Determination of federal policy at one level may markedly affect it at another level.

Relative to the principle of federal participation with the states in the financing of public education, the recommendations of practically all of the nongovernmental commissions within the last several decades have been in striking agreement. Examples are the following:

1. *The National Conference on the Financing of Education, 1933*— "there is variation in ability to support schools among the states. . . . This situation can be remedied only when a larger proportion of the school revenue comes from the Nation as a whole."

2. *The American Youth Commission, 1940*—"The Commission . . .

has debated this problem over a period of 6 years and has become convinced that federal aid is urgently required."

3. *The National Committee on Coordination in Secondary Education, 1941*—"The provision of federal funds for the partial financial support of education in the states is necessary and desirable, as a function of the Federal Government."

4. *The Interstate Committee on Postwar Reconstruction and Development, 1944*—"Control of education is a function of State Government . . . Participation by the National Government should be limited to financial aid and to providing leadership and information . . ."

5. *The National Citizens Commission for the Public Schools, 1954*—"Income taxes and sales taxes . . . levied both by the States and by the Federal Government . . . could provide the money needed to meet increased education costs without interfering with the operation of our economy."

6. *The Rockefeller Panel on Education, 1958*—"Federal programs in education now exist on a large scale . . . It is certain that they will increase both in scale and in variety. It is a stark fact that there are educational problems gravely affecting the national interest which may be soluble only through Federal action."

Of special relevance to this study is the report of the Commission on Financing Higher Education, created by the Association of American Universities. The Commission published its conclusions in 1952. Concerning the question of federal support for higher education the Commission said in part:

> It is the most important single question with which this commission has been faced. . . .
>
> The aid given by the government to the education of veterans has been justly acclaimed as a wise, proper and beneficial program. . . .
>
> Secondly, we believe the nation has greatly benefited from the services performed by institutions of higher education in managing research enterprises of critical importance to national defense. . . .
>
> Thirdly, we recognize the benefits to higher education and to the nation which have resulted from government support of the education of scientists and of basic research in agriculture and the natural sciences.
>
> Nevertheless . . . this Commission has reached the unanimous conclusion that we as a nation should call a halt at this time to the introduction of new programs of direct Federal aid to colleges and universities. We also believe it undesirable for the government to expand the scope of its scholarship aid to individual students.

Policies in International Education

The government of the United States, in cooperation with other countries, has also engaged in international education. Its activities therein may be classified as follows: (1) the bilateral relations entered into by the United States government under its own coordinated national program of educational and cultural cooperation with other countries; (2) the educational relations in which the United States government participates as a member of or contributor to international organizations, such as the Pan-American Union; and (3) after World War II, the relations between this country and the defeated nations for their re-education in the ways of democracy.

The basic governmental policy in this field has been to foster mutual understanding, appreciation and respect. Congress and several Presidents have contributed to its evolution and implementation.

For many years, educational and cultural relations with foreign countries have constituted one phase of United States foreign policy. And within the last few decades our government, like those of other countries, large and small, has placed increasing emphasis on such activities.

The Convention for the Promotion of Inter-American Cultural Relations, signed at Buenos Aires in 1936, was a forerunner of the first broad-scale, international educational program of the United States. In accordance with this treaty, we have exchanged two graduate students a year with each of the sixteen other signatory American republics.

Congress has authorized various activities in educational exchange with other nations. Such activities have included the exchange of special information and materials, the interchange of specialists, professors and college students, and cooperative educational programs.

By the Fulbright Act, signed by President Truman in August, 1946, some of the currencies and credits of other countries acquired by the sale of surplus property abroad were made usable for educational exchanges. The Act established a Board of Foreign Scholarships to select grantees and supervise the exchange. In broad terms the Smith-Mundt Act of January 1948 prescribed major international informational and educational exchanges. The India Food Aid Act of 1951 authorized educational exchanges between the United States and India, financed from sums payable by the government of India to the United States as interest on emergency food loans. These and other Acts affecting international exchanges, principally at the higher level, have been administered by the Department of State.

An important development in educational exchange became known on January 27, 1958, when the Department of State announced an agreement between the United States and the Union of Soviet Socialist Republics to exchange graduate students, university instructors and professors.

An Executive Order of May 9, 1955 made the International Cooperation Administration a semi-autonomous agency in the Department of State, and transferred to it the functions formerly administered by predecessor agencies. Education has always been an essential ingredient of the technical assistance programs of the ICA, since the basic purpose has been to provide technical training and know-how to other countries. Thousands of persons annually have received assistance.

On October 22, 1953, the President gave to the newly created United States Information Agency a statement of mission including certain educational activities such as library services, exhibits, lectures and guidance to students through binational centers abroad.

PARTICIPATION IN INTERNATIONAL ORGANIZATIONS

Besides its own bilateral activities in this field, through membership in the International Bureau of American Republics and in the Pan-American Union which developed from it, the United States government has participated in inter-American educational exchanges since 1906.

In London during November, 1945, the concept of international education received a great impetus. Delegates from the United States met with those from forty-three other countries to draft a permanent constitution for the United Nations Educational, Scientific and Cultural Organization. The Constitution came into force when adopted by the governments of more than twenty nations the following year. The charter provided for detailed activities in fulfilling the general functions of (1) collaborating in the advancement of mutual understanding of peoples; (2) giving fresh impulse to popular education and to the spread of culture; and (3) maintaining, increasing and diffusing knowledge.

In 1946 a joint resolution approving United States membership in UNESCO passed both houses of Congress and was approved by President Truman. The resolution authorized a national commission to maintain liaison between UNESCO and the government and private voluntary groups in the United States. Thus the foundation was laid for continuing participation by the United States government in the UNESCO work on all levels of education. Our government now contributes to the support not only of UNESCO but also of a number of other international organizations carrying on educational activities.

RE-EDUCATION AND EDUCATIONAL RECONSTRUCTION

Two major problems of the United States government in international educational relations emerged from World War II: (1) the reconstruction of the educational systems of the war-devastated countries, and (2) the re-education of the defeated nations in the ways of democracy. Interested governmental and nongovernmental agencies of the United States and certain allied countries cooperated for the accomplishment of these purposes.

In 1946 the Commission for International Educational Reconstruction was set up from a series of conferences called by the American Council on Education to consider the critical educational problems in the war-devastated countries. The Commission undertook the task of stimulating and coordinating American voluntary efforts to aid education in these countries. In the meantime the Allied Military Government had assumed supervisory and advisory functions in education in the occupied areas. Later, Allied re-educational policy placed increasing responsibility for revival and reform upon the native educators themselves.

Although ultimately the choice among ideas and procedures had to be made by the peoples of the occupied countries, educational guidance from other countries helped clarify the issues. Altogether, educational reconstruction and re-education in the defeated countries was an extraordinary accomplishment by international cooperation.

Scholarships, Fellowships, Traineeships

The historic background of certain federal programs, such as the "Regular" NROTC, regarded by some persons as scholarships, has already been set forth.

The "Regular" NROTC differs markedly from the "Contract" NROTC and from the Army and Air Force ROTC programs. Each year the Navy selects approximately 1,600 high school seniors for four years of college in the "Regular" NROTC. Each person is free to select his field of study and during the academic year receives $50 a month besides tuition, fees, books, instructional equipment and uniforms. Upon graduation, the "Regular" enrollee is obligated to accept a commission in the Regular Navy or Marine Corps and serve at least three years on active duty.

The federal government has also promoted manpower development through other scholarships, fellowships and traineeships, particularly in the sciences. The National Science Foundation Act of 1950 created the National Science Foundation for a number of purposes, including the following related to higher education in the sciences: (1) development and encouragement of a national policy for the promotion of basic research and education; (2) awarding of scholarships and graduate fellowships; and (3) providing a central clearinghouse for information concerning scientific and technical personnel.

In 1952 the Foundation started giving fellowships. Through grants for the support of basic scientific research the Foundation has also indirectly aided a large number of graduate and post-doctoral students performing research services for the grantee agencies or institutions.

Under the provisions of the Atomic Energy Act of 1946 (amended in 1954) the Atomic Energy Commission established small numbers of fellowships in radiological physics in 1948, in industrial medicine in 1949, and in industrial hygiene in 1952.

Federal research fellowships in public health began with the passage of the National Cancer Institute Act of 1937. As other national institutes of health have been activated they have also organized research fellowships or traineeships or both. Related to these was the provision by the 84th Congress of graduate traineeships to increase the supply of public health specialists and the number of professional nurses to teach or supervise other nurses.

With Title IV of the National Defense Education Act of 1958 came appropriation of "such sums as may be necessary" to reduce the shortage of qualified college teachers. The Act took two approaches: giving money to graduate students, and increasing the number and scope of graduate programs. The Office of Education allotted 1,000 fellowships for the first year of operation.

College Housing Programs

Under an extension of the Lanham Act of 1941 the federal government began assistance to college housing on a temporary basis.

The Housing Act of 1950 authorized the Housing Administrator to borrow up to $300 million from the Treasury to support long-term, low-interest-rate loans to colleges and universities for the construction of dormitories and faculty housing. The legislation represented Congressional recognition of a critical, accumulated need for on-campus residential facilities for the fast-growing enrollments of the institutions. However, because of the advent of the Korean conflict the program was suspended in July 1950. Subsequently a program limited to $40 million of borrowing was activated to serve the most acute needs arising from defense or defense-related activities.

By the housing amendments of 1955 federal loans were continued to colleges and universities for dormitories and certain other housing. This authorization was increased to $500 million in 1955 and to $750 million in 1956 ($100 million to be lent for service facilities such as dining rooms and student unions). In the 1957 Housing Act the Congress boosted it to $925 million, including $25 million for housing for student nurses and interns.

The maximum term of a loan has been fifty years. Junior colleges are eligible. Loans are administered by the Housing and Home Finance Agency through direct government-college transactions. The Office of Education provides educational advisory services.

At the close of 1959, loan funds for college housing were exhausted; and it was expected that in 1960 the Congress would consider new college-housing legislation.

Other Historical Policies and Programs

This historical review cannot note all federal activities in or affecting higher education, but only some of those most indicative of the development of relevant federal policies. Some of the more significant developments not already covered are the following:

(1) The need of Congress for information led to an appropriation for a library as early as in 1800. The published materials purchased during that year became the nucleus of the Library of Congress. Through the years the Library has primarily served Congress, but secondary services to executive agencies, the American public and the world of scholarship are growing. The collections and services have been particularly useful in advanced research.

(2) In 1867 the Secretary of the Treasury was authorized to receive a residuary legacy of James Smithson, an English scientist, "to found at Washington, under the name of the Smithsonian Institution, an establishment for the increase and diffusion of knowledge among men." In an address before the American Historical Association in 1888, Dr. G. Brown Goode emphasized the educational value of the National Museum, under the administration of the Smithsonian Institution. Through exhibits, exchange of publications with other countries, advisory services and in many other ways, the Institution has fostered knowledge. It has been especially helpful to advanced scholars.

(3) In 1879 the Congress began to make annual appropriations to Howard University, a privately controlled institution devoted primarily to the education of Negroes. Federal funds now constitute the main

support of Howard, over which very limited supervision is exercised by the Department of Health, Education and Welfare.

(4) With authorization of $7,500,000 annually for five years, the Library Services Act of 1956 provided temporary federal aid to states for extension of public library services to rural areas. Estimated to serve at least 27 million persons each year, the appropriations contribute to education at all levels.

(5) The Eighty-fourth Congress, through Public Law 813, authorized appropriations for encouragement and assistance to the states in the establishment of state committees on education beyond the high school. This was in connection with the work of the President's Committee on Education beyond the High School, in 1956 and 1957. Public Law 813 was the first of its kind. It set a precedent for federal aid to the states for the conduct of conferences on educational problems of national concern.

Current Policies and Programs

In the preceding pages we have considered the historical development of federal policies and programs in or affecting higher education—in general, and in particular forms, such as education for national defense.

This brings us to the question: What are the policies and programs currently in operation?

It was stated in the introduction to this essay that the federal government has no comprehensive policy on what it should or should not do in higher education, or, for that matter, in education at any level. However, a review of the scores of current federal policies and programs would be voluminous. It is feasible here only to list a representative number of the principal, current ones.

DEPARTMENT OF HEALTH, EDUCATION AND WELFARE

(1) Administration of the basic statutory function of the Office of Education, serving all levels of education.

(2) Administration of federal endowment of land-grant colleges and universities.

(3) Administration of federal funds for the federal-state vocational education program, which includes training of teachers for vocational subjects.

(4) Administration of federal funds for extension of public library service to rural areas, affecting all levels of education.

(5) Administration of national defense loan program for undergraduate and graduate students.

(6) Cooperative research program of the Office of Education—contracts with colleges, universities and state education agencies.

(7) Administration of the national defense graduate fellowships program.

(8) Contracts with institutions of higher education for operation of national defense counseling and guidance training institutes.

(9) Strengthening instruction in modern foreign languages—including contracts with colleges and universities for operation of language and area centers, research, and studies.

(10) Research and experimentation in more effective utilization of new media for the benefit of education at all levels.

(11) Grants for the improvement of statistical services of state educational agencies—affecting all educational levels.

(12) Participation in international teacher exchange programs including seminars abroad for American teachers.

(13) Training in education for certain foreign nationals.

(14) Providing international organizations information on education in the United States.

(15) Operating Gallaudet College for deaf persons.

(16) The financial support of higher education, especially for Negroes at Howard University.

(17) Allocation of federal surplus property for health and educational use—largely by colleges and universities.

(18) Provision of intern and other training in specialized medical fields at Saint Elizabeth's hospital.

(19) Financial aid to the states for vocational rehabilitation of disabled persons, involving education at all levels.

(20) Financial aid to states for the education of state and local public health personnel at secondary and higher education levels.

(21) Graduate and undergraduate training grants by the National Institutes of Health.

(22) Direct training by the Public Health Service for persons having doctoral degrees in certain sciences.

(23) Operation of the Public Health Service research fellowship program.

OFFICE OF THE SECRETARY OF DEFENSE

(1) Operation of the U. S. Armed Forces Institute—offering correspondence courses, elementary through college level.

DEPARTMENT OF THE ARMY

(1) Operation of the joint service National War College and Industrial College of the Armed Forces—instruction mainly at university graduate level.

(2) Operation of the Army service school system—elementary to college graduate instruction.

(3) Operation of the United States Military Academy—a degree-granting college.

(4) Administration of the Reserve Officers Training Corps—secondary and college level education.

(5) Operation of the Army Reserve School System—college undergraduate and graduate level.

(6) Training of military personnel, mainly college graduates, in civilian colleges and universities.

(7) Training of civilian personnel of the Department—secondary and college level courses.

(8) Contracts with colleges and universities for research and development of military weapons and methods—mainly graduate work.

(9) Operation of a program of general educational development of military personnel—junior high school through college graduate study.

DEPARTMENT OF THE NAVY

(1) Operation of naval service schools for military personnel, including the Naval War College, the United States Naval Academy, and the Naval Postgraduate School—providing secondary through college graduate education.

(2) Undergraduate and graduate training for military personnel in civilian colleges and universities.

(3) Departmental training of civilian personnel—secondary, college and graduate level.

(4) Training of civilian and enlisted military personnel to become commissioned officers in the Navy and Marine Corps—principally at the college level.

(5) Education of Marine Corps personnel through correspondence courses—provided by the Marine Corps Institute.

(6) Research and development carried out at colleges and universities —mainly graduate work.

DEPARTMENT OF THE AIR FORCE

(1) Administration of the Air Force Reserve Officers Training Corps— undergraduate college education.

(2) Provision of professional education for officers at the Air University.

(3) Operation of the Air Force Institute of Technology—courses mainly at college undergraduate and graduate level.

(4) Operation of the Air Force Academy—a degree-granting institution.

(5) Training for civilian employees—secondary school and college undergraduate and graduate courses.

(6) Operation of an Extension Course Institute providing correspondence courses for Air Force personnel.

(7) Contracts with colleges and universities for research and development—mainly graduate work.

DEPARTMENT OF AGRICULTURE

(1) Cooperative agricultural extension service, operating through the land grant colleges—providing secondary and higher-level education.

(2) Agricultural research service, carried out in connection with the land-grant and other colleges and universities.

(3) Forest service research in cooperation with institutions of higher education—findings utilized primarily by professors and students at these institutions.

(4) Agricultural marketing demonstrations and other educational services in connection with land-grant and other colleges and universities—principally at secondary and higher education levels.

(5) Agricultural informational services including preparation of publications, exhibits and motion pictures—educational at all levels.

(6) Providing facilities for the Department of Agriculture Graduate School.

DEPARTMENT OF COMMERCE

(1) Training of employees, including "out-service" training at colleges and universities.

(2) Training of certain foreign nationals under provisions of the Mutual Security Act—at college undergraduate and graduate levels.

(3) Operation of specialized training schools, including the United States Merchant Marine Academy, a degree-granting institution, and the National Bureau of Standards Graduate School.

(4) Contracts with colleges and universities for research.

(5) Financial aid to degree-granting state marine academies.

(6) Payment of college tuition and related fees for selected employees.

DEPARTMENT OF THE INTERIOR

(1) Operation of management training and development programs for certain employees, including graduate courses at universities.

(2) Under the Mutual Security Program, providing college-level training of foreign nationals in scientific and technical activities.

(3) Cooperation with colleges in fellowships to expedite research projects of the Department.

(4) Financing undergraduate and graduate engineering courses at colleges for certain career employees.

(5) Cooperation with land-grant colleges in wildlife research.

DEPARTMENT OF JUSTICE

(1) In-service training of employees—at secondary and professional levels.

(2) Operation of the Federal Bureau of Investigation National Academy—post-secondary training for state and local law enforcement officers.

(3) Elementary, secondary and higher education for inmates of federal penal and correctional institutions.

DEPARTMENT OF LABOR

(1) Promotion of apprenticeship and other industrial education at secondary and higher levels.

(2) Secondary and college-level staff training, including aid to state agencies, by the Bureau of Employment Security.

(3) Secondary and post-secondary-level training of state safety inspectors and other personnel by the Bureau of Labor Standards.

(4) In-service training of employees of the Department—at secondary and postsecondary levels.

(5) Technical education of certain foreign nationals, under agreement with the International Cooperation Administration—involving contractual services of institutions of higher education.

POST OFFICE DEPARTMENT

(1) Management development seminars for some employees—secondary and higher level education.

(2) Operation of the Postal Inspector Training School—instruction at professional and graduate school level.

TREASURY DEPARTMENT

(1) In-service training of employees, including operation of United States Customs In-service Training School—education at secondary and higher levels.

(2) Operation of the United States Coast Guard Academy—a degree-granting institution.

(3) Coast Guard training for officers and enlisted men—secondary and higher level education.

(4) Coast Guard reserve training—including utilization of institutions of higher education.

DEPARTMENT OF STATE

(1) Administration of the international educational exchange program of the United States—involving college graduate and undergraduate students, primary and secondary-school teachers, university lecturers and advanced research scholars, specialists and leaders.

(2) Administration of the international cultural presentations program of the United States—including some artistic and athletic presentations having their origin in institutions of higher education.

(3) Negotiation and facilitation of educational exchanges with countries of the Soviet bloc—participants being university students, professors and specialists.

(4) Foreign Service Institute training given to Foreign Service Officers and certain other employees of the Department.

INTERNATIONAL COOPERATION ADMINISTRATION
(A semi-autonomous agency within the Department of State)

(1) Training foreign nationals in the United States and third countries—about one-third of the participants being enrolled in institutions of higher education.

(2) Providing cooperating countries with United States technical advisers—who perform technical and higher educational functions.

(3) Technical assistance to educational systems and institutions in cooperating countries—at all educational levels, including university-to-university contracts.

(4) Financial support of some educational institutions, at all levels, in a few cooperating countries.

NATIONAL SCIENCE FOUNDATION

(1) Promotion of education in the sciences—including (a) fellowships for further training of graduate students and teachers, (b) institutes for supplemental training of teachers, (c) special projects in science education, and (d) projects for improvement of science courses at all levels.

(2) Grants for basic research in the sciences, principally at colleges and universities.

ATOMIC ENERGY COMMISSION

(1) Contracts for research and for training in research—arranged with industrial establishments and with universities.

(2) Award of a limited number of fellowships in certain sciences.

(3) Operation of the Oak Ridge Institue of Nuclear Studies, and an International School of Nuclear Science and Engineering—principally higher education.

VETERANS ADMINISTRATION

(1) Payments to veterans pursuing education—largely in colleges and universities.

(2) Payments to educational institutions of all levels for records and reports on education of veterans.

(3) Support of vocational rehabilitation for disabled veterans—involving education at all levels.

(4) Payments to war orphans between 18 and 23 years of age pursuing education in vocational schools and colleges.

HOUSING AND HOME FINANCE AGENCY

(1) Lending to colleges and universities for student and faculty housing.

(2) Interest-free repayable advances to state and local governmental agencies for advance planning of non-federal public works, including institutions of higher learning.

UNITED STATES INFORMATION AGENCY

(1) Operation of a worldwide informational program involving close working relationships with universities, including financial support of American studies in foreign universities.

(2) Administration of a program promoting the sale of American books and other informational media—serving education at all levels in cooperating countries.

(3) Provision of language and area training of Agency foreign service officers at the Foreign Service Institute of the Department of State and at selected universities.

SMITHSONIAN INSTITUTION

(1) Administration of United States government exchange of scientific, literary and governmental publications with foreign governments, institutions, and investigators—subservient to education in general but mainly higher education.

(2) Exhibition and informational services of the Bureau of American Ethnology, National Air Museum, National Collection of Fine Arts, National Gallery of Art, National Zoological Park and United States National Museum—educational at all levels but particularly aiding advanced scholars.

GENERAL SERVICES ADMINISTRATION

(1) Participation with the Department of Health, Education and Welfare in distribution of surplus real and personal property to health institutions, schools, colleges and universities.

(2) Loan of machine tools in the National Industrial Reserve to secondary and higher educational institutions.

(3) Administration of the general activities of the National Archives and certain Presidential libraries—especially aiding college undergraduate and graduate students.

OTHER FEDERAL AGENCIES

(1) *National Aeronautics and Space Administration*—Contracts with universities for research, utilizing university staff and students.

(2) *Small Business Administration*—Cosponsorship with colleges and universities of short courses in administrative management.

(3) *Tennessee Valley Authority*—Administration of research and educational programs in agriculture and forestry, carried out in cooperation with the land-grant colleges and other agencies.

(4) *Civil Service Commission*—Promotion, conduct and coordination of federal interagency training programs, involving all levels of education.

(5) *U. S. Government Printing Office*—Cataloging, indexing and distributing public documents, educational at all levels.

(6) *Federal Reserve Board*—Participation with graduate schools of several universities in conducting seminars on economic and monetary problems.

(7) *Federal Aviation Agency*—Provision of educational programs for Agency personnel in engineering, management, and other fields—including special courses at colleges and universities.

(8) *Library of Congress*—Administration of the general activities of the Library which are educational at all levels but which especially aid advanced scholars.

DISTRICT OF COLUMBIA

(1) Operation of public schools and other educational institutions including a teachers' college.

(2) Provision of in-service training of personnel of the public welfare, police and other departments—secondary and higher education.

(3) Administration of special programs of health education for the public—instruction at all educational levels.

Conclusions

From this historical study a number of conclusions emerge, the following among them.

The policies might be classified in several ways. First they might be called either "permanent" or "temporary." Federal support of the land-grant colleges is continuing and presumably permanent, whereas aid to students provided by the National Youth Administration during the depression of the 1930's, and operation of the Army Specialized Training Program during World War II, were temporary.

In his survey of federal activities in higher education after World War II, James E. Russell considered the policies as relating to either (1) the federal government as educator, including instruction for federal personnel and for nongovernmental individuals; or (2) nonfederal higher education, including relationships to institutions and to individuals.

With respect to underlying purpose the policies might be classified as pertaining to (1) the national defense, (2) the promotion of public health, or (3) other specified purposes.

For the Commission on Financing Higher Education (1952), Richard

G. Axt placed the major federal programs in three categories, namely: (1) aid to special groups of individuals and to individuals in special fields of study; (2) federal grants and contracts for research at universities and colleges; and (3) annual federal grants to particular institutions for purposes other than research. Such categorizations contribute to an understanding of the several policy developments.

An outstanding conclusion from this study is that there is no single department or agency which has an overall responsibility or even co-ordinating authority for carrying out federal policies in higher educa-tion. The Office of Education (which might be supposed to have such authority) is only one of a large number of agencies administering pro-grams in this field. From a study for the Commission on Organization of the Executive Branch of the Government, Hollis Allen found that only one percent of federal funds expended for education in the fiscal year 1949 was channeled through the Office of Education. Later studies have shown this percentage continuing very small.

In some instances two or more federal agencies have cooperated in the administration of a particular educational program. There has been, however, no general cooperation of the federal departments and inde-pendent agencies in the administration of federal educational activities. Frequently a large educational program has been administered quite independently by a single federal agency.

It is apparent that in education, as well as in some other fields, the nation has not been so much concerned with comprehensive organization as with satisfying special needs or interests. Federal agencies desiring to utilize education or educational institutions for special purposes have obtained diverse authorizations for a variety of higher-educational programs without evident regard for broad federal policy. Some consoli-dations of administration have been made and others attempted. How-ever, a number of the separate programs in higher education have be-come deeply rooted historically, and there are strong forces in favor of maintaining their independent administration. Furthermore, the close relationship of many of the programs to the broader functions of the agencies administering them raises serious questions of the feasibility and practicality of consolidating the administration of these educational activities. Certainly, however, the feasibility and desirability of further coordination is considerable.

For many years there has been great diversity in the in-service train-ing policies of federal agencies. A few have had no in-service training programs. Others have had elaborate formal programs for the training of personnel, civilian and military, including the operation of institutions of higher education up to the graduate level. Others have had authority to enter into contracts with non-federal institutions, including colleges and universities, for the training of personnel. Altogether the multiplicity of authorizations for various types of in-service training programs among the agencies has evidenced no consistency of federal policy. However, since 1938 the Civil Service Commission has promoted, conducted and coordinated some interagency civilian employee training activities. The Government Employees Training Act of 1958 became the basic authority for intra-agency, interagency and out-service (including college and university) training of civilian employees of virtually all agencies of the federal government.

There has been no blanket legislation giving all federal agencies similar authority to enter into contracts with colleges and universities for research. Also there has been no overall legislation governing the geographical distribution of such contracts. According to information obtained from some agencies, they have awarded their contracts to institutions judged best equipped to perform the desired services. The question of what other considerations may have influenced the awarding of such contracts is open to further study. Many of the largest federal contracts have been given to some of the nation's largest and most heavily endowed universities. This fact has raised the question of the effects of federal payments to educational institutions upon (1) the stronger and the weaker colleges and universities, and upon (2) the geographical distribution of opportunities for higher education in the United States.

Federal payments to colleges and universities, for whatever purpose, have had important indirect as well as direct effects. The choice of a university by hundreds of veterans, for example, may have been influenced by their knowledge of the existence of superior educational facilities at that institution. These better facilities in turn may have resulted in part from the use of federal funds paid to that institution for purposes other than the education of veterans.

On the other hand, some universities have declared that they have received no financial gains from fulfilling federal contracts. Whether the contracts have, as a whole, tended to make "the rich richer and the poor poorer" among the institutions might be an appropriate question for investigation.

For a number of years higher education in the United States has been receiving a large measure of its support from federal funds. In the academic year 1958-59 between one-sixth and one-fifth of the income usable for educational and general purposes by institutions of higher education came from federal sources. This does not include transfers of federal surplus property or direct federal appropriations for building purposes. Federal payments to the institutions now consist principally of those for the further endowment and support of the land-grant colleges, and payments made under contracts for research and for the training of federal civilian and military personnel.

Generally the federal programs are for the accomplishment of educational objectives of federal agencies which are promotional to the primary functions of those agencies. This study has revealed little evidence that the primarily non-educational federal agencies administering higher-educational programs have been particularly concerned about the effects of their respective programs on higher education in general, although these effects have been far-reaching.

In this connection it might be pointed out that the many service training programs have considerable general educational value for the nation. They lift its educational level, even though they are designed for specific purposes of the administering agencies.

Following is a brief summary of some of the characteristics of federal policies that have evolved to date:

(1) There has been no general policy governing what the federal government should or should not do in higher education.

(2) Federal activities in this field have generally been subsidiary to (although often also basic to) the performance of other federal functions, such as provision for the national defense, or promotion of public health.

(3) The federal programs have been largely for the higher education of special groups, such as military personnel, veterans, and federal civilian employees.

(4) The federal programs have emphasized the teaching of particular subjects, notably military science, the natural sciences, agriculture and engineering.

(5) Directly through fellowship awards, and indirectly through contracts with institutions for research, federal programs have provided financial aid to a number of graduate students.

(6) Federal policies have advanced "practical" research, particularly in the physical, biological and medical sciences but have given little direct aid to theoretical research in the social sciences or in the humanities.

(7) The federal policies have encouraged vocational and professional rather than liberal education.

(8) Federal policies have produced a great variety of procedures in the administration of federal higher-educational programs, sometimes involving relationships of a primarily non-educational federal agency with hundreds of educational institutions.

(9) Although mainly promoting training for particular groups,

federal policies have also encouraged higher education for large numbers of people.

(10) Federal policies have in the main promoted publicly controlled rather than privately controlled education.

(11) United States policy in international education has constituted an important phase of the foreign policy of the government.

3.

Federal sponsorship of university research

♦ James McCormack

♦ Vincent A. Fulmer

In their basic functions American universities are modeled after those of Western Europe. By contrast, however, American universities, both public and private, maintain a strong tradition of service to the general community, a tradition distinctly American in origin. In this country the formulation of university goals has been conditioned to a large degree by rapid national development and practical dependence upon scientific progress to promote economic and political growth. This link with the mainstream of everyday events in turn has had important consequences for the structure of American universities and for their relations with the federal government.

76

♦ James McCormack, Major General, USAF (Retired), is Vice President of Massachusetts Institute of Technology. While on active military duty, General McCormack served, among other capacities, as director of military applications, U. S. Atomic Energy Commission; and director of research and development, U. S. Air Force.

♦ Vincent A. Fulmer is Director, Industrial Liaison Office, and Executive Assistant to the Chairman of the Corporation, Massachusetts Institute of Technology. A former teacher of economics, he is a member of the Operations Research Society of America and the Institute for Management Sciences.

The Universities and the Federal Government

The practical role of American colleges and universities in promoting economic progress and in developing an enlightened body of citizens is as old as the institutions themselves. Within the last twenty years they have been asked to play a new and critical role in national affairs. The fact that they could be utilized to promote national security ranked in importance with the discovery of America's phenomenal ability to expand industrial production during World War I. What was conceived as a wartime mobilization of colleges and universities has now become a permanent part of the life of many of these institutions. As the functions of government, both military and civilian, come to depend increasingly upon complex scientific information, the use of university resources has grown steadily. Some prominent examples are in the provision of technical assistance to less-developed countries, the extensive use of university personnel in government advisory committees, research and development sponsored by federal agencies, the cultural exchange programs of the Department of State, and the education of government military and civilian personnel.

The most rapid growth in government-university cooperation has been in federal grants and contracts to underwrite research. In 1940, for example, the government provided $15,000,000 in grants and contracts to colleges and universities for research and development. Almost all

77

of this was for agricultural experiment stations of the land-grant institutions. Two decades later the estimated federal expenditures for "on campus" research will be $462 million in fiscal 1960. Total federal expenditures for research and development have risen from $74 million in 1940 to an estimated $7.5 billion in 1960—a hundred fold increase.

Prior to World War II most of the scientific needs of the federal government were accommodated within the government framework and within government laboratories themselves. With the exception of agricultural colleges and a few specific programs (such as land grants and ROTC), the federal government did not sponsor institutions of higher learning to any extent. When not supported by private means, those institutions were generally thought to be the proper objects of interest of the states. In the early history of the United States the domination of the private institutions precluded any significant federal role in higher education.

The government went beyond its own laboratories to seek large-scale assistance for the first time from colleges and universities in World War II, mainly for military applications of nuclear energy, communications, control systems, and improvements in propulsion. Industrial resources for these fields were not as available then as today. The universities were successful in bringing science and engineering to bear upon problems of military technology; they were willing and eager to contribute to the war effort. Their achievements have in turn greatly influenced their relationship with government in the postwar period.

The postwar emergence of the United States as a world leader brought enormous responsibilities in international affairs. In seeking resources to meet this challenge, the federal government again appealed for assistance from the colleges and universities—in trained manpower, advice, and prosecution of research. The cold war and Soviet achievements in space technology have further accelerated this dependence.

In examining the research relationships between the government and universities, one immediately faces a bewildering complexity of organizational forms in the agencies which provide the funds. In the aggregate the agencies reflect the complex and multi-purpose functions of the federal government. But their variety of purpose and structure presents major difficulties in generalizing government-university relationships in research. For example, the National Science Foundation recently noted that almost half of the 80 organizations which make up the executive branch of the federal government were engaged in scientific activities in 1953-54, including research and development in their own laboratories. Moreover, federal agencies have virtually a free hand in determining a number of policies that are as important to universities as the substance of research itself. The size of grants and contracts, their placement in an academic, industrial or governmental setting, and the substantive content of research programs are almost entirely the responsibility of the federal agencies under present legislation.

A variety of research relationships has been developed, each of which differs somewhat in purpose and character. Federal agencies and the universities have pursued their mutual interests in such ways as to include university-wide commitments, subdivisions of universities, individual faculty members, and even students themselves on a direct basis. There are joint undertakings in which several federal agencies combine to sponsor collaborative research in one institution or several. There are also differences according to the manner in which research relationships are affected by statutory or contractual provisions.

It is clear that government sponsorship of university research is stimulating conspicuous changes within higher learning, changes which deserve thoughtful and informed study in order to appraise their significance.

The Role of University Research

Research, in various guises, has always been a part of higher education. Teachers with a more-than-average grasp of current knowledge, have naturally displayed a more-than-average interest in expanding that knowledge; and the arts and substance of teaching have invariably benefited. But the past gave us scant preparation in this respect for the past few decades, where discovery and development have come to follow each other at such a pace as seemingly to deny us the opportunity to understand the new before we must learn something even newer, and sometimes confusingly different from all that has gone before.

Without suggesting that classic principles are overturned daily through research, it is clear that the growth of our understanding of things and happenings in nature sheds new light on those principles (and occasionally does overturn one). And the quicker the rate of change, the deeper the importance of close relationships between research and advanced teaching.

Of course not every teacher is or should be a research scholar, nor is every scholar a teacher. The two bents are by no means identical. They may run parallel, but not all people are doubly gifted, or interested. It suffices for science and education that individuals have the opportunity to exercise their talents in both, and that we encourage good research for the value to science of the results and for the stimulation of education in science.

From the national point of view, such indeed is the joint interest of universities and the federal government in university research. However, one can go too far in building on this obvious truth. The university, no matter how genuine its interest in seeing its research serve the needs of society, must in dedication to its primary responsibility give greatest emphasis to its teaching function. Government, on the other hand, while recognizing its responsibility for education, must shape its sponsorship to give due emphasis to national needs for research results—in atomic power, in military weapons, in weather prediction, and so on. The emergence from university research of a new idea for improving electronic communications, for example, can be important to the government if it serves no other purpose. But the university can be fully satisfied only if the result also serves the educational process—if it improves the value of a teacher, stimulates a student, adds to knowledge.

Thus the joint interest, however natural in the usual case, does receive somewhat different emphasis from the two parties. It is when this gap opens too wide that fears are most urgently expressed regarding the compatibility of sponsored research with the objectives of academic institutions. Actually, the central incompatibilities are not severe and can, with understanding management, be turned into strengths. Society would be the loser if government administration failed to use university research resources or proceeded to use them without comprehending the educational forces which dominate the academic community. The university would be the loser if it seriously inhibited the access of its science and engineering faculty and students to the powerful technologies of our time, in which government support is often crucial to meaningful participation.

At this point, in view of the variety and complexity of operations and issues, it is well to pause for a few definitions. The means of supervising and financing government sponsorship of university research takes several forms, and the methods of university participation cover a wide range. It can be misleading to generalize about administrative practices that range from the management of a large off-campus laboratory to the coordination of a typical small project in a teaching department. To give some preliminary focus to the more detailed discussion to follow, therefore, we present a brief outline of the principal variants, and hope that succeeding comments may be identified with the scheme to which they pertain. Let us first consider the government side.

Probably closest to the prevailing image of the government scheme is the system of grants employed by the National Science Foundation, mainly in the physical sciences, and by the Department of Health, Education, and Welfare in the life sciences. The basic idea is to strengthen the fundamentals of science generally while emphasizing certain areas in accordance with technical significance and financial need. Within available funds, grants support worthy endeavor where competent individuals are ready to take responsibility for its supervision. The result is a broad spread of funds, institutionally and geographically—broad in comparison with the concentrated "mission-oriented" research, connected, for example, with certain military programs.

Grants are made on the basis of proposals from individuals and groups, supported by their institutions. The size of the grant is determined through estimated direct costs of time, materials, and services, frequently supplemented by funds to pay for part or all of needed special equipment. To the total is then added a percentage, generally fixed by law or regulation,* of direct costs to be applied toward the institution's indirect costs: building maintenance and repair, utilities, and other items of general administrative expense.

A second system for financing government sponsored university research is represented by the contracts commonly used by the "operating" agencies of government, of which the Department of Defense, the Atomic Energy Commission, and the National Aeronautics and Space Administration supply the most familiar examples.

It is possible to philosophize on the difference in spirit between grants and contract payments for financing research, but in truth the fundamental difference is not so great. Present law permits a number of government agencies to make grants as an alternative to contracts, and the decision between the two methods tends to be in large part a matter of agency practice or management detail, for example, affecting the ownership of special equipment. A grant by definition permits operating flexibility, but so also can a contract when the contracting agency so desires.

Further back in the government organization and fiscal cycle, as annual budgets are being approved, there is close scrutiny of the research to be sponsored by the various agencies; and a mission-oriented department, such as Defense, must justify its sponsorship of a given scientific area in relation to its missions: in weapon development, oceanography, intelligence, or whatever. The resulting programs, conducted mainly under contract, are properly weighted toward applications rather than toward basic research. But properly also, a large amount of basic

---

* At least, such has been the case. The National Science Foundation is now urging within government the application to grants, where practical, of negotiated charges for indirect costs as is done with research contracts. This will be discussed in some detail later.

research in relevant scientific areas is sponsored by the military establishment (see Table 1), and where it parallels research supported by grants from the National Science Foundation, for example, there is little difference to a university if both programs are intelligently administered. By the nature of research, a contract can hardly call for a more specific result than would come in the same case from a grant, nor can the contract instrument in any magical way fix the course of the research or the date on which pre-ordained results will emerge.

The amount of the contract is based, as in the case of the grant, on an estimate of the direct cost of the project. Additional allowances, however, are negotiated, unlike the common present procedures for grants. Typically, the government and the university agree on a guide-line rate at the beginning of the fiscal year to cover the pertinent parts of the university's operations during the year. Then, at the end of the year, when actual costs can be presented, the figure is renegotiated to a precise amount.

TABLE 1

FEDERAL SPONSORSHIP OF BASIC RESEARCH
(Obligations Basis) Fiscal 1959
(Dollar Figures in Millions)

Agency	*Amount*	*Percent of Total*
Department of Defense	$117	24%
Atomic Energy Commission	98	20
National Aeronautics and Space Administration	88	18
Department of Health, Education, and Welfare	73	15
National Science Foundation	59	12
Department of Agriculture	29	6
All other agencies	29	6
Total	$488	100%

Source: National Science Foundation, *Federal Funds for Science, VIII,* Washington. GPO 1959.
Note: Percentages and dollar figures do not equal totals because of rounding.

Thus far we have dealt with government methods for sponsoring research on campuses, predominantly as a departmental activity of the university although occasionally interdepartmental, in all cases an integral part of the academic process if not everywhere a specific part of current teaching. The third and last method we shall mention is the employment of university management for the operation of large laboratories. Here, the university resources sought, in addition to physical management, are the integrity of a responsible public trust and the attraction of a university to professional laboratory staff.

We shall return later to this type of effort. It is mentioned here to emphasize that although it accounts for almost half the government funds flowing to universities, it lies apart from the matters to which we give principal attention in the interaction between science and education.

So much, for the time being, for the variants in government procedure. We shall turn now to a brief description of the principal methods by which universities accept these funds and the responsibilities they entail.

First, we shall mention the relatively small and personalized project in which a principal investigator, with one or a few associates and minimum administrative support, undertakes a line or research, estimating its duration and specifying the funds required. Typically, his assistants will include graduate students who may be working to supplement their income or to acquire background for a thesis or other technical paper. Typically also, the project proceeds from the earlier work or interests of the investigator and uses equipment and supplies —even perhaps some money—left over from such work. The operating funds allocated by the government may be augmented from other sources available to the university. The group may include persons from more than one department, but the project is generally identified with a particular department. The reports coming from such work are given as wide distribution as circumstances permit and their importance merits. In short, the arrangements are businesslike but not tightly formalized.

Projects of broader scope, especially with two or more departments involved, may be supervised by a higher administrative echelon of the university, but the next large step is likely to be found where work of a more continuing nature and requiring substantial financing seems to require a laboratory of indefinite tenure. Here, the university is gambling on continuing support from outside and therefore gives close attention to the size and scope of the endeavor as it implies commitments beyond the period of assured project funding. Such laboratories may be departmental or interdepartmental. They may be significantly endowed from other than government funds. They may, as in the past with agriculture at some places, form the nucleus of a school. Such, indeed, may be the future course of recently emergent areas of interest, as for example in the interacting physical, electrical, and chemical properties of materials. At least, the possibilities are of great interest to education, both broadly and, as regards each institution, in the context of its own position and prospects.

The financial aspects of these laboratories are of long-range interest also to the government administrator. Where competence is organized on a continuing basis, especially where it encompasses related disciplines, the commitment for continued support rests not with the university alone but with all who have pertinent responsibility for strengthening research and for amplifying and implementing its results. Thus, the government administrator sees his future funds subject to an increasing and most persuasive call, which, however beneficial in other respects, will certainly pass to universities and laboratories some fraction of his present authority for detailed selection among individual projects and for shifting support from one individual or institution to another.

Beyond this sort of laboratory, in size and philosophy, lies the large laboratory operated by a university for the government. Some examples are: the Los Alamos Laboratory, by the University of California for the Atomic Energy Commission; the Jet Propulsion Laboratory, by the California Institute of Technology for the National Aeronautics and Space Administration; and the Lincoln Laboratory by the Massachusetts Institute of Technology for the Air Force in behalf of the military departments. The pattern of these laboratories, and certain extensions of the pattern, mark an acceptance of public responsibility which opens a somewhat separate set of questions of accommodation to university organization. The connection with learning is real; the connection with teaching tends to be thin, although not always negligible. The matter deserves special attention, and we shall return to it.

Thus, universities respond in a variety of ways to the national need for research, as they are requested, encouraged, or enabled. One must add to the variants we have outlined, concerning mainly the mechanics of administration, others of personality and imaginativeness in this highly individualistic business of research *cum* teaching.

There is no really standard form. The administrator who feels uncomfortable among such complexities is well advised to turn his attention to other fields.

EDUCATIONAL CRITERIA

We have pointed out that research is essential in the educational process. There are, of course, colleges and universities which do not encourage research to any great extent. Indeed, at institutions where it plays a prominent role, a sizable fraction of faculty members do not participate. The fact remains that such institutions and faculty still benefit from the search for new knowledge conducted elsewhere or by others.

When research is sponsored it expresses a mutuality of purpose between sponsor and recipient. An abstract view of the university might lead one to conclude that influences by the sponsor upon the direction or selection of study are an interference with academic freedom. This view is closely linked with an antiseptic concept of university life and presupposes a predominantly passive character in the make-up of institutions of higher learning. History indicates otherwise. Great universities have always concerned themselves with the urgent problems of their time. Sponsored research is a desirable aspect of university life, not because it is free of basic conflicts, but because the area of mutual interest between sponsors and universities far overshadows the area of conflict. It is the search for a common ground between institutional objectives and those of the sponsor which concerns us here.

In this, a central question revolves around the criteria by which the university will accept or reject a research program. Two main considerations should be satisfied. First, the university must be free to determine independently whether a research proposal contributes to or detracts from the role it sees for itself. Whatever it does, the university will not want to depart from its primary function as an educational institution. This principle of self-determination is not only essential to the prosecution of a research program, but also vital to the preservation of the institution itself.

Second, if research is to be valid in an academic setting, it should be motivated by educational objectives and not narrowly by a specific end-use of the knowledge sought. Using this standard, the choice of research at a university is bound to be influenced by the character of education there, as well as by the nature of the disciplines represented. Institutions which emphasize the teaching of fundamentals are more apt to favor basic research over those whose objectives are primarily vocational.

In the aggregate, the division of university research between basic and applied is weighted on the basic side, although applied research and development are by no means excluded. For example, the National Science Foundation has estimated a 64-36 split between basic and applied research on the nation's campuses in fiscal 1954.* The Committee on Institutional Research Policy of the American Council on Education has commented on this division of university research as follows:

In our society educational institutions are the principal sponsors of basic research and uncommitted scholarship. They

---

* National Science Foundation, "Scientific Research and Development in Colleges and Universities, Expenditures and Manpower, 1953-54," Washington, GPO, 1959.

therefore have heavy responsibility to encourage the free exercise of intellectual curiosity as their special share of the nation's research activities of all kinds. At the same time they should not be limited by any narrow or doctrinaire definition of what is appropriate research. We believe that fine distinctions between basic research and applied research are difficult to draw. Investigators should be free to pursue that kind of research which contributes best to their educational objectives and to the fields of investigation they embrace.*

The use of categorical definitions to segregate research which universities should or should not perform is likely to generate more heat than light in the selection process—even if workable definitions of basic and applied research were available. The practical difficulty of applying these definitions has led educators to de-emphasize the semantics in favor of such educational criteria as: Does the proposed research contribute to the professional development of the principal investigator? Is it suitable as a possible thesis topic for interested students? Does the area of study represent an area of university competence? In practice, almost all universities engaging in sponsored research are equipped to do applied research, and many do so either from a sense of public duty, or because of faculty preferences, or in consideration of sponsors' interests. This is not to say that universities live in an ideal world. Most of them would prefer to place more emphasis upon basic studies if financial support were available in the amounts and areas needed.

The evaluation of sponsored research in an academic setting is usually stated in terms of praise and criticism of present systems of sponsorship. These arguments have been stated more often in form than in content. Objections to "projectitis," lack of control by university administrations, amount of time required by faculty members to do research at the expense of time spent with students—these and allied questions are not in opposition to the basic concept of research on the university campus. Such criticisms are sometimes aired by those who place only a nominal value on the regenerative effect of sponsored research and are more impressed with the shortcomings of the present system than its advantages.

Research, properly viewed in the universities, is not an appendage to the educational process; it is an organic means through which basic university goals are related and reinforced. In theory and practice the concept of federally sponsored research is workable. It is, in fact, a key

---

* Report of the Committee, 1954.

to future growth and attainment in American institutions of higher learning.

Project Selection and Administration*

The processes by which universities and their faculty members select the research they would do—and find sponsorship for—could serve as material for interesting studies ranging from high (and low) finance to campus politics. Our interest here is limited to some procedural matters and to a few of the substantive issues of the effect of government research sponsorship on relationships between government and education.

An educational institution is a decentralized enterprise. In contrast to the more authoritative forms of organization of government and industry, the university is at the other end of the spectrum with regard to decision making. Decisions bearing upon the academic life are made at all levels of faculty and administration. This is not to suggest that there is no exercise of institutional authority, but simply that in an intellectual community professional decisions are initiated on an individualistic basis. Students themselves participate in this decentralized order by their choice of academic subjects and of topics for thesis investigation. They are in turn conditioned by the values held by their parents and by their intellectual environment. Alumni, trustees, and visiting committees bring further significant influences to bear in all phases of university operation. The organizational make-up of the university thus involves a complicated interplay between faculty, students, parents, committees, department heads, deans, other university officials, and those who serve on a part-time basis.

To fulfill their essential functions, institutions of higher learning require freedom in both their administrative and academic pursuits. In the selection of research projects this means that individuals can best contribute when they are free to argue whether a subject is worthy of investigation. Even if faculty members were willing, it would be foolhardy for an administration to pose as authority on problems that should be studied. The identification of a problem is an integral part of the investigation itself and must be done by the individual. In research, there is no substitute for the individual's knowledge and judgment.

---

* In this section the authors were greatly assisted by the comments of Mr. Richard W. Pratt, Director, Office for Research Contracts of Harvard University. He is not responsible for the opinions we state, but they are surely wiser for his counsel.

When research is sponsored by a federal agency, there are three parties to the selection of a project: the faculty member or group proposing the project; the interested agency; and a university organization which must provide a setting for the conduct of the research. The final selection requires that each play a role in determining the desirability of a particular project at a particular institution at a given time. The individual can contribute his specialized knowledge in the formulation of plans and objectives. The government agency is interested in sponsoring research to cover the development of a field related to its responsibility. The university must insure that the project fits its criteria, that it is worthy, that it is consistent with the educational pattern of the institution, that it can be accommodated by the physical and administrative facilities.

With funds for support, the government agency can wield positive influence in pointing up the relevance of a research proposal to the national need and in revealing plans for similar undertakings at other institutions. The agency frequently has information about research activities in a general field which may be of value in determining whether research of a particular type can best be conducted at a given institution.

The institution itself must provide a balance among alternative research possibilities on its campus. Once in possession of a proposal by a member of its faculty, the university must decide whether the research makes sense in terms of its capabilities and chosen lines of development before placing it formally with the sponsoring agency. Usually, the machinery for arriving at this decision will include the faculty member himself. Approval or disapproval is thus a matter of meeting certain institutional criteria. Beyond these, the individual is free to pursue his research as he sees fit.

Individual faculty members will be self-disciplined in advance through previous exposure to the scrutiny and accomplishments of their colleagues. Despite this element of control, however, an institution's portfolio will inevitably contain at any given time projects less desirable than others. To be effective, any selection system should allow for its own imperfections, especially one which is used to discriminate among research proposals in an academic setting. "Unproductive" research is not by definition a waste. "Unproductive" lines of inquiry frequently provide as sound a basis for new directions as those projects which result in positive findings. The inefficiencies of university project selection can thus take two forms: the freedom of the individual to choose research methods which lead to poor results, and another which is purely administrative—a small but certain number of marginal projects from time to time.

ADMINISTRATION

Under today's procedures, the time required for preparation and defense of research proposals is a shortcoming. To some extent the effort here is inescapable in view of the increasing complexity of science and engineering. It is hard to find someone better qualified to defend a proposal than its originator. The fact remains that there is an urgent need for improved methods to minimize the demand on faculty time. The nature of research itself suggests that proposals be flexible and permit maximum latitude. The need for flexibility is further emphasized by the heterogeneous settings of university research. For federal agencies this of course poses problems of designing a system to take account of the wide variety of educational institutions without discarding the advantages of uniform treatment of all where appropriate.

Sound policies for sponsoring university research are basic factors of organization. Their success depends upon the ability of federal agencies to attract and hold competent individuals in positions of importance and to permit them discretion in university relationships. A government science administrator aware of the wide differences among educational institutions can encourage or discourage the conduct of government sponsored research. If he is sensitive to conditions at an institution, he can exert a positive influence on the conduct of research there. In matters of procedure he can save himself, the university administration, and the faculty member a great deal of harassment by the thoughtful application of government standards and procedures.

In turn, it is incumbent on a university to organize its research administration in a manner compatible with the magnitude of the financial commitment. When a goverment representative appears with a heavy briefcase full of contractual "boilerplate" to apply to a $5,000 basic research endeavor, the university is negligent in its duty to society if it even allows him a chair to sit in while making his argument. On the other hand, universities do not have the right to ask government agencies to install separate memory sections in their electronic business machines to accommodate a completely different bookkeeping system at every institution. Nor can a university leave the business and financial management of sponsored research projects to be handled between the government and the individual investigators. The university has a responsibility to shield its scientific staff from the harassments of unfamiliar administrative detail. It has no less a responsibility to protect the government from outrageous idiosyncrasies. It has a responsibility to insure that its books will stand up under audit; that its patent policy protects the institution and the individual along with the government; that expenditures accord with the budget approved in good faith; and so on.

The representatives of government may be depended upon to insure that academic freedom does not expand into management license. But the university, in its own research interests as well as in consonance with its responsibilities as a public trust, must not leave to government alone the task of making sure that traffic flows smoothly in a street that must always be two-way.

The university gladly accepts responsibility for the professional excellence of its research. It assumes the right (properly) to expect financial support for the work it wishes to undertake, and it demands freedom (again quite properly) from interference that might prejudice the technical quality of the work. It accepts equally the obligation not to be more of an administrative nuisance than is absolutely necessary.

Research Centers

A successful innovation of the Office of Scientific Research and Development during World War II was the creation of university research centers. The universities undertook to supply management for the assembling of scientists and engineers for concerted attack on areas of major technical importance with specific end purposes in view. The Applied Physics Laboratory of Johns Hopkins University, which developed the proximity fuse, was one such endeavor. A second was the Jet Propulsion Laboratory, for rocket development, by the California Institute of Technology. A third was the Metallurgical Laboratory at the University of Chicago, which developed the basic uranium and plutonium technology. A fourth was the Radiation Laboratory at M.I.T., which developed radar.

The practice was followed by the Manhattan Project, with the Los Alamos Laboratory operated by the University of California. The pattern was continued and extended after the war by the Atomic Energy Commission and the armed services, resulting examples being the Lincoln Laboratory for air defense research, a descendant at M.I.T. of the Radiation Laboratory, and the atomic weapons laboratory at Livermore, operated by the University of California. A variant is the Brookhaven National Laboratory for work in atomic science supported by the AEC and operated by an association of universities, the management of which has since undertaken also to build and operate a radio astronomy center for the National Science Foundation.

These are examples of the larger ones. There are a score of others, generally smaller. Some have disappeared or folded into successor organizations.

The motivation in each case was a national need that in government's opinion could be adequately met only by the universities. Although the full course of this organizational development may not yet have been run, it would seem, under present circumstances, that the trend would be in other directions. The existence now of well-rounded research and development capabilities in industry and in non-profit organizations not directly university managed offers the government other resources adaptable to such missions. Some of these organizations have been initiated by universities, although as corporately separate entities, such as Cornell Aeronautical Laboratory and Stanford Research Institute. Two, at least, were created specifically to take responsibility for the more industrially oriented parts of the operation of a university managed center: The Sandia Corporation, relieving the Los Alamos Laboratory, and The Mitre Corporation relieving the Lincoln Laboratory.

Obviously, we have been witnessing an important evolution. The university solution was the initial catalyst, and has generally worked well. It has caused philosophical and administrative difficulties, both for the government and for the participating universities, but the satisfactions of national service have generally outweighed the troubles.

These centers are large and require extensive facilities. The work in some of them is dangerous. So they are generally located off-campus. Their missions require that they have considerable authority to deal directly with their sponsors in setting and carrying out their programs. Secrecy enters also as a segregating factor, for much of their work is classified. These and other considerations have led typically to a substantial degree of autonomy in both administrative and technical affairs.

As a consequence, then, of a degree of separateness, the programs of the centers are not related to education in the close sense used mainly in these pages which deal with on-campus associations. It should be noted, however, that wherever possible the managing universities promote intellectual relationships between their faculties and the professional staff of the centers. Depending on the activity in the center and its distance from the campus, this effort succeeds in varying degree. In some places it is quite successful.

The importance of these centers, as they have evolved in some instances from their original quite specific purposes, is that they serve as "institutes" for the concentration of a wide range of talents toward broad yet concerted objectives. In this concentration they perform a service beyond that which campuses can supply. They also entail certain risks for the universities.

Because of their size, their financial operations are large compared with other university activities. Because they must compete in the market place for staff, lacking some of the university's attractions, their salary scales are above campus levels. Other costs tend to run higher also, from operating closer to the industrial world. The result, with large cash flow and higher "unit costs," is an inflationary influence in university finances. Perversely, the closer the relationship of the university with the research center (for the advantages to the center of technical support and competent managerial supervision) the more effectively the inflationary influence can operate. And in any case, where the center's budget is large compared with the university's other operations, a management mistake that permitted a sizable fraction of center costs to fall back on the university could be serious indeed.

There is a challenge also to the university in that the center, with a position of eminence and a degree of intellectual monopoly in its field, is subject to forces of complacency. If as a consequence its quality deteriorates, the potential embarrassment to the university is obvious. The insurance of quality is in the main achieved through the environmental infusion of the university's own uncompromising standard of intellectual excellence. Yet the necessarily large measure of autonomy granted to the center for the conduct of its technical affairs conditions the university's ability to guarantee the result.

The principal advantages accruing to a university from its managerial role in one of these enterprises stem from the fact that the work of the center is genuinely important (else the university has no business being there). So, first is the satisfaction of public service, which is not negligible.

Second, and somewhat more tangible, is the association afforded to schools of science and engineering with some of the dominant technologies of our times. Despite the sometimes casual attitudes displayed by faculties and students in this regard, there can be no real question as to the values of association with work of major technical importance.

Third, and most tangible, the center provides a source of qualified specialists for teaching, particularly in advanced subjects: for part-time and term assignments, for lectures, for conducting seminars—sometimes for permanent transfer to the faculty, when the individual is qualified and so moved. The center, in turn, can offer stimulating off-period work for faculty members, occasional support for on-campus research, and job opportunities for students and new graduates.

As regards interchange of faculty and center staff, there are of course some inhibitions. A university cannot permit either its administration or its on-campus work to profit financially from the university's control of the center. Similarly, it must police the time and compensation of faculty members participating in the center's work to insure that no special privileges are enjoyed. And, in the reverse direction, salary differentials introduce difficulties into the employment of center staff as teachers.

However, on the whole, with careful and intelligent direction, these inhibitions are modulated and, provided the separation in distance or nature of the work is not too great, the interaction can bring positive benefits to both sides. Indeed, such must be the case in the long term. When duty has been done, the university has no cause to continue in the management of such operations unless it can enhance quality and, at the same time, strengthen educational processes.

Secrecy in Research

Among the issues in government sponsorship of university research, the matter of secrecy has contributed its share of troubles. Taken as including clearances to work on classified research—with the judgments on individual loyalty and reliability that are involved—this general question of "security" has reached deep into the principles of university administration as well as the emotional bases of academic freedom.

The strategic importance of science in such critical matters as radar, fire control systems and the atomic bomb led to the erection of secrecy barriers within and around the scientific community at the beginning of World War II. These barriers were designed to keep research of military importance secret and to insure the discretion of the scientists in it. In this difficult field—the balancing of the national need for military security with the scientific tradition of freedom to seek and disseminate knowledge—previous experience in our country was largely non-existent. It was inevitable that universities and their scientists should find the introduction of secrecy a complex responsibility.

The most acute difficulties arose following the discovery after World War II of celebrated cases of espionage in the atomic energy centers of the United States, Canada and Great Britain during the wartime atomic energy work. The troubled history of the loyalty-security program thereafter was part of the problem posed by the changed relationship of government to science, and the academic community's share was amplified by the American phenomenon of extensive application of university research to the national security.

Perhaps the most important lesson from this experience is that the security and prosperity of the United States, depending as they do on progress in science and technology, do not permit a degree of secrecy that critically hinders the race or denies for long to the public an understanding of its nature and objectives.

Secrecy systems pose a number of practical restrictions on university campuses quite apart from the intellectual restraints. Many have a high nuisance value which a scientist, with instinctive distaste for locking doors on science, finds it easy to exaggerate or resent. Some are expensive in money and working space. Few university buildings are designed with secrecy in mind, and the result can be a distortion of the natural location of campus research. Classified projects often leave a residue of classified information that must be kept under surveillance after a project has terminated, with universities sometimes finding themselves the uncomfortable custodians of material that they can neither use nor dispose of promptly.

Understanding the need for secrecy, universities have played a leading role in pointing up the relevance of specific research programs to military operations. Disagreements generally occur not on need for secrecy but on where to draw the line, and it is natural for the university to oppose the extension of secrecy restrictions to programs and results that, in its view, might better be left unclassified. While some universities have chosen peace and quiet by declining to perform classified research during peacetime, others have taken a larger share of responsibility for national security as represented by classified research undertakings on their campuses. These latter institutions have involved themselves in a hard search for ways and means to manage classified research so as to minimize its handicap and to limit its disruptive effect on unclassified activity. Indeed, much of the progress in defining, segregating, and declassifying military research can be attributed to the determination of a few universities to face up squarely to the problem.

Associated with the security classification of work is the security clearance of persons for reliability and loyalty. At an early stage in the development of the necessary procedures, new to government and citizen alike, all contractors, including universities, were expected to take responsibility for clearing their own staffs for the lower degrees of classification. This ruling was in due course withdrawn for educational institutions. The government now holds the sole responsibility for determining whether university staff members should have access to classified information including, of course, participation in classified research itself.

UNCLASSIFIED RESEARCH

A more serious difficulty related to the now half-forgotten demand that participation in any research receiving government support, even if unclassified, be subject to certain loyalty standards.

In 1955 the National Science Foundation took the lead among federal agencies in urging the elimination of the loyalty test as a prerequisite to receiving government funds for research in unclassified areas.

In the same year a committee of the National Academy of Sciences reviewed the matter of loyalty in government sponsorship of unclassified research. In March, 1956, the committee submitted a report pointing out a number of ill-defined policies and practices of the federal agencies. The committee recommended that:

> (1) The test in the award of grants and contracts for unclassified research should be the scientific integrity and competence of the individuals responsible for carrying out the research, and the scientific merits of their program.

> (2) When an official of the government comes into possession of evidence which in his opinion indicates existence of disloyalty in violation of law, he should promptly refer that information to the federal agencies of law enforcement established to deal with such matters.

> (3) An allegation of disloyalty should not by itself be grounds for adverse Administrative action on a grant or contract for *unclassified* research by scientifically competent investigators; if the indications of disloyalty appear sufficiently serious to warrant any action at all, the government in the opinion of the committee has no other course than to bring formal charges and to produce the evidence in open hearing before legally constituted authority.*

These summary findings and recommendations contributed importantly to a new pattern among the federal agencies which have followed in principle the suggestions of the National Academy of

---

* Press Release of April 4, 1956 from The White House, by James C. Hagerty.

Sciences committee. To a certain extent the committee's work reflected the progress already made in loyalty considerations in government sponsorship of unclassified research. To a much larger extent, the committee's work contributed to bringing order into previous chaos. Thus, personal loyalty checks within educational institutions are now limited to performers of classified research, and the responsibility for security clearances is in government hands.

The general situation, however, continues, and presumably will so continue indefinitely. Clearly, many people feel there is an overriding need for loyalty in higher education. From this point of view, the educator, because of his influence on the young at a crucial stage of intellectual growth, must expect special attention to be paid to his motivations. The educator instinctively senses an entering wedge of prejudice to academic freedom, an old story to universities. He also resents being singled out from other citizens for potential attack of questionable inspiration. At the least, he demands that the law be clear so that the public may understand the rules, and that the process of accusation and trial be judicial and removed from partisan politics. As is well known, meeting these demands will take time. We may be heartened, however, by the progress we have made away from the climate of fear, suspicion, and uncertainty which followed the first public realization that we had a new and dangerous kind of traitor in our midst.

The latest episode happens to include not faculty members but students. The National Defense Education Act of 1958 requires that recipients of student loans sign an affidavit stating that they neither have supported, nor were a member of, certain organizations defined as subversive. The loans are based on the principle of university participation at the rate of one dollar for each nine dollars provided by the federal government. Thus, the new loyalty requirements under the NDEA apply not only to the government's portion but also to that of educational institutions, making the universities loyalty oath administrators. A number of colleges and universities consequently have declined to participate in the new NDEA loan program until the loyalty oath provision is resolved. In May, 1959, the Secretary of Health, Education, and Welfare recommended the repeal of this provision to the Congress, and the proposal has strong support in both the Senate and the House of Representatives. As of this writing, however, no Congressional action has been taken.

The difficulties posed by secrecy on university campuses are not matched in industry. In his book, *Government Contracting in Atomic Energy*, Richard I. Tybout describes an attempt to determine whether atomic energy contractors have found it difficult to work under secrecy controls. In recent field studies conducted by the Atomic Energy Commission, there was found to be some objection to the delay caused by clearance procedures in putting new employees to work; otherwise, opinions differed. Some atomic energy contractors even pointed to practical advantages of secrecy systems. Security controls are useful as administrative systematizers, they reported, in such matters as the circulation of documents and the orderly entrance and exit of visitors and employees in restricted areas. Moreover, personal security clearance helped form an efficient working organization. The explanation was that employees with a record of poor conduct on the job are inhibited from applying for security clearance because of the close scrutiny of personal integrity and character.

DECLASSIFICATION

In the fiscal year 1959 federal agencies obligated a total of $686 million for research in educational institutions. $383 million or some 55 percent was placed at educational institutions proper, and the remainder was for research centers administered by the universities. Of the $383 million, it is estimated that between 10 and 15 percent is for classified research on campuses. Within the research centers themselves, it is difficult to obtain an estimate of the classified fraction of their total research, but it is certainly substantial. By the assignment of a large amount of classified work to these centers, national need has been met while reducing the difficulties which would otherwise have been imposed, at least in part, on campuses.

Secrecy remains in basic conflict with the role of universities in generating and disseminating new knowledge. In the short run, the problem can be greatly reduced through improved techniques for early discernment of research that can be declassified.

Over the long term, with care not to prejudice important government requirements for research in the field of national security, reduction of classified work on campuses must be sought through: (1) development of intellectual resources outside the educational system capable of undertaking classified research now performed by the universities; (2) increased emphasis on research as opposed to development on university campuses; and (3) increased awareness in government that basic research, a key to national survival, does not flourish in secrecy.

In Chart I, earlier consideration of the subject matter and objectives of the research project might have permitted its declassification well before the imaginary date of completion. In real terms the earlier discernment of unclassified subject matter could greatly reduce the

CHART I

STEPS IN DECLASSIFICATION OF A RESEARCH PROJECT

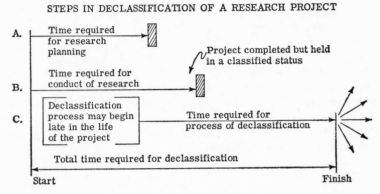

amount of university research that is held either in a classified or indefinite status until work has been completed and published. A great deal of progress has been made in this direction; more is needed.

Publications

A primary objective of government sponsored research in educational institutions is to generate information. Thus, federal agencies have been generous in the allowances made for publication of results. An estimated five percent of university research costs, or some $35 million, at the current level of federal sponsorship, is allocated to the preparation, production, and distribution of reports. Added to the cost of processing documents through such federal agencies as the Armed Services Technical Information Agency (ASTIA), the Office of Technical Information of the Department of Commerce and others, university publications have become big business. They are important not only because of the large sums of money but also because of the crucial role they play in stimulating scientific and technological advances in both education and industry. The publication of a technical report often represents the only tangible and immediate benefit received by the sponsor in return for financial backing.

In small research undertakings, the reporting may be limited to a single publication at the conclusion. In larger, longer programs, which include a number of inter-related studies, the practice of issuing progress reports has been widely adopted. The frequency, detail, and purpose of these reports vary considerably and are usually a subject for negotiation at the time a research contract is written.

The publication of research findings serves desirable ends for both the sponsoring agency and the university. From the agency's point of view, published information is accessible for industrial and governmental laboratories where applied and developmental work may be pursued on the basis of findings made within the university. Indeed, one of the principal advantages to the federal agency is the academic propensity to disseminate new knowledge promptly and widely. In contrast to work within industrial and governmental laboratories, where proprietary interests and military classification may inhibit the free flow of information, research in universities operates on a leverage principle that stimulates the widest possible participation of the scientific community. To the sponsoring agency, publications are also an invaluable means of gathering data for future decisions about sponsorship.

The classification of research reports is done at a price to the investigator, to his university, and to the government sponsoring agency. It is a part of the price of reducing the threat to freedom that, in the first instance, brings university efforts within forms of bureaucracy historically unfamiliar to the university environment. Reducing the unnecessary hindrances of secrecy is the preoccupation; reducing the need is the goal.

A NEW DIMENSION IN PUBLISHING

Government funds have helped overcome the publications log-jam that has grown steadily since the beginning of World War II. Under government sponsorship, many of the research reporting systems have been invaluable in transmitting findings in rapidly moving fields much sooner than if only the professional journals were available. In some extreme cases editorial backlogs in the standard professional journals are running as high as eighteen months. A good example of a federally financed *ad hoc* channel is the Atomic Energy Commission's publication program in nuclear physics, which supplements the standard professional journals.

On the other hand, the improvisation of new publications media under federal sponsorship has not reduced the demand for space in the standard journals. Paradoxically, it has increased it. Having reported their findings to the sponsor, university investigators are no less anxious to place articles in the professional press, it being clearly in their interest to do so. Frequently, a journal article is a means of publishing research which may have grown out of a government sponsored project but which does not fall entirely within the sponsor's support. Often the reporting obligations to the sponsor does not satisfy the investigator that the full import of his findings has been brought to the attention of the professional community. Some federal agencies have recognized the problems posed by double reporting and have permitted faculty members to publish their findings in a form which will satisfy both the sponsor and the professional press. Others have insisted upon special forms of reporting designed primarily to serve their purposes without much regard to the added work load. One effect of the resulting proliferation of scientific publications has been to bring the universities into publishing activities on a large scale. To the extent that scientific journals have become inadequate and sponsoring agencies require special reports, the universities have had to invent publication facilities for much of the expanded volume of scientific literature growing out of their own research.

The solution does not lie within the universities themselves, although further recognition by sponsoring agencies of the burden of excessive and overly detailed reporting can ease the problem for educational institutions. New techniques for documenting and disseminating scientific achievement will have to be devised to handle the tremendous outpouring of publications from the government's expanded sponsorship of research, both within and outside the educational community. These techniques will require significant changes in the nature and function of the professional press as we know it today.

People and Programs

ACADEMIC SALARIES

No new emphasis need be given here to the fact that salaries of educators have lagged seriously in the past twenty years. Efforts to raise them have generally been more successful during the past three or four years than previously, but the results are still unsatisfactory. "Lack of funds" sums up a host of reasons why this is so, some internal to higher education and others rooted in the values assigned to higher education in our society. Chart II displays some of these factors.

The unprecedented rise in research and development expenditures has brought stiff competition from industry and government not only for faculty members but also for technically educated students at all degree levels, many of whom have inclination and potential for teaching. The associate professor, five or more years beyond his doctorate, all too often watches a new Ph.D. he has just steered through the process, go to first employment at a salary exceeding his own.

Educational institutions with large commitments to science and engineering have been hard put to attract and hold enough first-rate faculty members. To the extent that a part of the salary can be charged against sponsored research, part of the burden of increases can be shifted from general funds to the research budget. However, this kind of financing, common in industry, appears as a risk in the psychology of a university, whether tenure salaries are involved or not, because of the short-term nature of most sponsored research funding.

CHART II

SOME FACTORS WHICH INFLUENCE FACULTY SALARIES

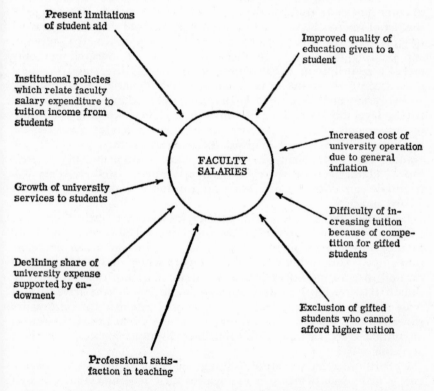

Some schools seek to minimize this risk by maintaining basic academic salaries at lower levels and providing incremental payments to faculty who engage in sponsored research during the summer or when teaching loads are less than full time. But if the payment of tenure salaries out of temporary research funds means financial risks for the university, the practice of financial reward according to participation in sponsored research has deeper implications. Aside from the short-term nature of these increments, the extra pay, combined with the uneven sponsorship among academic disciplines, tends to create faculty "haves" and "have nots" and to pattern the emphasis of the university to that of research sponsorship.

In its report on Government-University Relationships in Federally Sponsored Scientific Research and Development, 1958, the National Science Foundation urged against incremental salary payments to faculty engaged in sponsored research. Some schools have nevertheless continued extra pay on the ground that faculty are provided with incentives to enter into more research than they might otherwise do, accepting the conflict of interest between educational purposes and desire for personal income—with the attendant need for care in screening research proposals and policing the system. In their view, sponsored research not only makes a contribution to education, it has had a direct and practical effect upon their ability to maintain reasonable salaries. Both industry and government have created laboratories and working conditions comparing favorably with those of universities. These working conditions include opportunities to conduct research with many of the freedoms associated with academic systems. In some companies, personnel are granted leaves of absence to teach or pursue problems that interest them. Thus, comparative research opportunities as well as salary differentials can critically determine an institution's ability to hold its faculty intact.

In developing compensation policies, educational institutions have traditionally turned toward their own internal finances. In doing so they rely heavily upon the non-salary advantages of an academic community. One such advantage, the tenure system, has added much to caution in granting salary increases. Accustomed institutional rules of thumb relating faculty salary expense to tuition income have altered more slowly than the infusion of sponsored research into university education has changed the meaning of teacher-student ratios. Restraints on tuition increases have thus sometimes disproportionately restrained academic salaries.

Opportunities for private consulting and other professional endeavor enable many faculty members to augment their academic salaries as well as to gain experience that keeps them as teachers. At the same time, faculty consulting opportunities pose special problems. In particular, they are not uniformly available and are therefore difficult to take into account when setting salary scales.

In the administration of academic salaries, the single most important consideration is the *permanence* of promises. A tenure commitment is indeed serious for a university when a "chair" has half a million dollars of endowment.

Each institution has its own financial worries. Tax supported schools contend with the political pressures of the appropriations process; the privately supported are reminded by the bankruptcy that occurs from time to time in their midst that they operate under rigorous financial limitations. The entire community must fear the decline in effectiveness that goes with financial distress.

RESEARCH SALARIES

The employment of full-time, non-tenure, research staff is common at educational institutions having substantial research undertakings. Working in close association with faculty members who supervise projects and with students who may be part of a team, these individuals add to the quality and continuity of research. They are a principal means by which the changing requirements of research, personnel and money, can be accommodated without interfering with the instructional activities of the academic departments. From the project director's point of view, it is difficult to estimate from year to year how many students will be available and interested in associating with a particular undertaking. To the extent that full-time research staff is accessible, the faculty member in charge is also freed of many time-consuming aspects of experimentation; he can give more of his energy toward the formulation of plans and supervision. Supervision and stimulation are especially important with students whose association may be in the form of a thesis investigation for a graduate degree.

To those who accept non-academic appointments, the opportunity to work with outstanding faculty members in an atmosphere conducive to research is a significant attraction. The freedom to publish and to develop their own understanding of their specialization in an environment free from commercial interests or restrictive regulations is among the primary reasons for accepting appointments, often at financial penalty. The contributions of these staff members to faculty-student relationships and to the substantive content of research deserve a high order of recognition. Without their collaboration faculties could not be as productive in research and teaching. They represent an able and potentially large source of teachers to meet the expanded enrollments on the way for the 1960's. At institutions which encourage research they already play a vital role in the professional development of both students and faculty. Many are authorities in their own right and can pace rather than follow intellectual standards. Those inclined toward teaching are all the more effective for their personal association with laboratory and departmental research programs.

The readiness with which research staffs can be recruited is a matter of record. The conditions under which employment is offered and the way in which research personnel are integrated into the organizational complex vary with institutional policies as do project selection, details of contracts, and other aspects of sponsored research.

Research salaries, on the other hand, are influenced by external factors, and they present universities with questions of salary administration in which experience has been limited. Broadly speaking, research salaries are influenced by the level and structure of academic salaries on the one hand, and on the other, by the competitive behavior of the market for research manpower. Large-scale government sponsorship enables an institution to enter the market for personnel with scales which may be low because of the nonmonetary advantages of working in a university environment, but which are at least realistic.

In turn, this inflationary pressure is passed to the academic salary structure because of the internal relationship between academic and research salaries. Neither industrial nor governmental organizations are averse to recruiting faculty members and full-time personnel for leading research positions in their laboratories. An institution with large commitments can no longer enjoy the simple existence of determining salary policies in the light of compensation levels at other colleges and universities and by examining its own financial position. Research operations which comprise as little as 10 percent of the university's total budget bring with them the vicissitudes of the market place and the noneducational influences which contribute to the behavior of research salaries.

Employee benefits—health and accident insurance, life insurance, pension arrangements, and other supplements—are also part of the pattern. In view of prevailing practice, these salary supplements are important for both their competitive and intrinsic value. Because of them, academic compensation becomes even more closely tied to that for research personnel.

The large university-managed research center complicates salary administration. The provision of administrative services to the major research centers requires the enlargement of the general administrative function of the university. In the national interest, the university must support the programs at these centers by offering salaries and working conditions attractive to top-flight scientists and engineers. The result is a salary structure which differs from that on campus. Yet institutions which manage research centers typically place a heavy emphasis upon research in their own campus laboratories. Consequently, in accepting the responsibility for the centers, they take on the enlarged task of managing another separate but not entirely distinct salary system.

The search continues for management procedures which increase the availability to the center of the substance of the university without producing adverse effects on the nice balance of forces sustaining that substance.

FACULTY TENURE

However important such questions as salaries may be, they do not constitute the most basic consideration. With adequate funds and a reasonable attitude in federal administrators, institutions will devise ways of administering salaries to promote the advantages of a vigorous research program. By far the more important challenge to education growing out of federal funds for research is to insure that the changes they introduce in the university environment will enhance creative scholarship and educational effectiveness. One area requiring watchfulness is the effect of government sponsorship upon faculty tenure policies and practices.

Academic tenure, as an inducement to the teaching profession, is intimately related to the need of an institution for independence in its pursuit of truth, for continuity and excellence in the exercise of its educational function. In order to encourage faculty research, an institution must recognize accomplishment as one reason for the award of tenure. The terms under which research is sponsored have a direct bearing, therefore, upon the tenure system.

The award of tenure applies only to the institution which makes it and not to the entire educational community. The prerequisites for it on one campus may differ markedly from those on another, and the practices of granting it are necessarily affected by financial position. However, tenure almost always means a degree of security and recognition for the recipient, either locally or among his professional colleagues at large. The important feature, for present purposes, is the fact that academic tenure is not automatically self-regulating but is a principle of administration. As such, it is subject to subtle influence from university research relations.

Where research is a legitimate reason for awarding it, tenure is two-valued in contrast to that granted for teaching alone, and thus there are extra complexities. Proved researchers are more difficult to identify than proved teachers, and the proof is certainly not found in the quantity of research performed, even in the number of papers published. There is reasonable assurance that a good teacher will continue to teach effectively, but usually less certainty that a high level of research activity will be sustained. Where research is regarded as a large part of the educational process, constant vigilance is needed to insure that tenure practices do not discriminate against faculty members who engage in little or no research but who are nevertheless important teachers.

The submission of a proposal is an integral part of the conduct of the research itself. The identification of problems and the formulation of plans are not easy to delegate administratively. In order to do research, a faculty member must somehow find someone willing to sponsor it. Whether he himself looks for a sponsor or whether the institution does, the fact remains that his research must somehow be related to the interests of sponsoring agencies. It is necessary, therefore, to safeguard against the premium that may be placed on showmanship to the disadvantage of the capable scholar whose motives are genuine but whose persuasive ability is low.

Moreover, the relative ease with which developmental projects attract some kinds of government support can place a strain on a tenure system which recognizes research accomplishment. Where a project accepted falls below standard—and this risk increases with the greater urgency frequently associated with development, as opposed to basic research— it is more likely the educator who loses than the project. Where a graduate thesis may also be adversely influenced, the loss is compounded. Where a non-tenure faculty member may be involved for the sake of increasing his visible research volume in moving toward tenure, the loss is further aggravated.

At the 52nd meeting of the Carnegie Foundation for the Advancement of Teaching in November 1957, the trustees engaged in an all-day discussion of the education of college teachers. Their report ended with a number of recommendations, which included as a final point: "All institutions of higher learning should accept responsibility for the continued intellectual and professional growth of faculty members." *

The tenure system, protecting the right of dissent in the continuing exploration for truth and in its teaching is a vital prerequisite to the process. The fact of its principal deficiency—that it also gives a degree

---

* *The Education of College Teachers,* Page 18.

of protection to the unjustifiably complacent and the unworthy—only emphasizes the critical significance of taste and discernment in tenure awards. As sponsored research becomes a weighty factor in the system, the quality of its administration becomes very important indeed.

The Problem of Indirect Costs

The subject of this section is money—questionably the root of all evil but unquestionably both lubricant of the research machine and source of friction among its operators. These parties are principally the researcher, the sponsor's agent, and the university research administrator who shuttles in the middle ground. To expand the analogy—with a purpose more serious than the method—we might highlight a most important aspect of a nagging problem, that of indirect costs, by reporting three imaginary (or at least modestly exaggerated) statements of the difficulty, one by each of the principal operators.

First, let us hear the representative of government, Mr. Smith, speaking to the university research administrator, Mr. Jones.

"Mr. Jones, some of my colleagues would be appalled by your demands on behalf of Crossroads College, which they would consider as going beyond the delicate proprieties for a non-profit institution dedicated primarily to the education of our youth. For my own part, I am not appalled because I work a lot with universities and understand their financial plight. Indeed, I was saying just the other day to a friend of mine that the Department of Health, Education and Welfare has got to face up to the need for subsidizing education on a broad basis or else we are going to find ourselves second best to the Russians in educated people—of all things!

"But really, Mr. Jones, I am sure that as a reasonable man you can see there are definite limits to how far my department can go in subsidizing education in the name of sponsored research. Take the case of Professor Brown here, who is so widely respected that there can be no suggestion of any derogatory intent in my remarks. But let's look at the facts. Professor Brown has a project he wants to pursue. You consider it a good project on its scientific merits alone. More than that, the professor has a student who would like to build a Ph.D. thesis around the idea of the project, so teaching is benefited as well as science per se, and Professor Brown is benefited as a teacher. Moreover, you state that the professor has time to direct the project without neglecting his teaching commitments, that he has laboratory space available and research assistants ready for assignment to the project. In fact, everything is available to make the project go except for the money to pay the incremental costs to Crossroads College.

"Now it so happens that I agree with you in every respect on the merits of the project and am prepared to support it—and not just in the amount of the incremental direct costs but also for a fair share of your indirect costs. Unlike some government agencies which allow as indirect costs only an arbitrarily fixed percentage of direct costs, which is too low, my department has me sit down with you and work out your actual costs, both direct and indirect, in accordance with the law and our regulations. I have, for instance, at your request, allowed a fair fraction of Professor Brown's salary which, being a tenure salary, could well be considered one of your fixed academic commitments. I have gone beyond that in allowing a proper fraction of the salary of his department head and dean who will devote some of their time to looking over Professor Brown's shoulder on his project. Your administrative and property maintenance costs are covered, in proper proportion.

"Actually, the specific, incremental, direct cost of this project is only $10,000: $6,000 for direct non-tenure salaries and wages and $4,000 for equipment and special supplies and services. To this I have added $2,000 for a share of tenure salaries and $4,000 for related indirect costs, bringing the total to $16,000.

"Would you not agree, Mr. Jones, that you would be out some $3,000 or $4,000 of this amount in any event—in your normal operations—without this project? I regard the difference between $10,000 and $16,000 as a reasonable contribution to your excellent institution to assist in maintaining its property and the quality of its staff and to continue in the front rank of research and teaching.

"Now we both know that a comparable effort at XYZ, Inc., would come at a higher price, so I want to eliminate two potential false arguments right away. First, we want to support this project at Crossroads because of the quality of Professor Brown's proposal and not because your costs are less; we do not buy research on lowest bid. Second, XYZ and Crossroads represent two entirely different cost situations. At Crossroads, research goes along happily with teaching, you have tenure and academic freedom, you are tax-exempt and receive gifts and grants for education and research from any sources, which are considerable, although I join with you in wishing they were larger. This project to you, in simplest terms, is a useful adjunct to your main mission of education. At XYZ, on the other hand, research is business. They have to compete. This means that they have to hold their costs to reasonable levels, and we make sure that they do. But it also means that we must pay them a fair price, to enable them to keep their facilities modern and to attract and hold good people. For this we pay them a fee, as well as reimbursing their direct and indirect costs, because the country needs many good XYZ's just as we need many good Crossroads."

Mr. Smith rests his case, and we turn to Mr. Jones.

"Your statement, Mr. Smith, would appall some of my colleagues who would say that you are ducking the real issue of the national values of research as an integral part of education while displaying a general lack of understanding of the university process. But not I, Mr. Smith, for I have worked a lot with government, and I understand rather well your need for separating more sharply than we do the things that are Caesar's from those more closely related to the spirit and mind of mankind.

"None of my arguments here relate to why costs are higher at XYZ, which, incidentally, is a first rate research organization. Moreover, I agree that their price should be still higher relative to their identifiable costs, for they must have a fee, which would be entirely unsuited to a project such as this at a university. I would agree also that you can give no weight in your administrative scales to such bonuses as the new Ph.D. which the work helps Crossroads add to the national inventory. These questions touch on issues of deep national significance (whither our colleges?) but they are not our principal concern in this particular discussion. My argument is simply this—that in a strictly business sense, your rules should permit you to recognize all of the valid elements of costs at both places. Maybe you fall short at XYZ—I don't know—but, if so, I know that you fall shorter in our case. Let's look at a couple of the elements.

"At a nonacademic institution, you look at the organization as a whole in deciding on allowable overhead. The personnel function, for example, is accepted as contributing in proper proportion to all activities it supports. Yet at an academic institution it is ruled that the academic budget must bear such costs for all academic personnel. The amount of money involved may not be enormous, although it is not negligible to us, but the principle is very important because it contributes to the setting of a false basis for other calculations that involve very large sums. For example, in the matter of facilities you make allowance to XYZ for amortization of physical plant which, taking into account tax write-offs is of the order of, say, 10 percent per year. In our case you allow 2 percent of book value. Translated into standard commercial practice, this would mean a 50-year amortization period. Seriously, does anyone believe that today's research facilities will be even remotely relevant to the tasks of the year 2010?

"In carrying out the research job that the country needs done—that we want to do and that you want us to do—Crossroads is a slave to the forces of a tidal wave far beyond our ability to control or even to modulate substantially. Let me illustrate.

"In 1940 we had a faculty of 200 and an academic budget of $5 million. We spent $200,000 on research—a sizable figure for those days. Today, with a faculty twice the 1940 size and an academic budget four times the 1940 figure, we spend twenty times as much in research.

"You see, Mr. Smith, our research no longer ambles along at the modest level which once permitted the non-sponsored costs to be covered by appropriations from the general funds of the college. Neither we nor the country would want it now to be so restricted. Yet we must be able to cover our costs somehow, or end in bankruptcy just as surely as any other business operated at a loss.

"You say that we are non-competitive, and indeed we are, in the profit sense. But I say that we are competing with the most inexorable of forces: deterioration of our facilities and, ultimately, of our capability as we fail to make ends meet.

"Could we not then just forget philosophy and agree that in one respect universities are altogether like all the other organizations with which you deal—that is, they must break even, and in the necessary absence of budget surpluses available for reassignment from other elements of their operation, their research must bear its share?

("We should move along quickly, Mr. Smith, for I don't really trust this roof. But softly, for I don't trust the floor, either.")

During this discussion Professor Brown has worn an increasingly bemused expression. He now has an opportunity to speak, as follows:

"I have heard you two gentlemen with patience and some understanding, and I do agree that indirect costs are important—indeed vital in the end. However, right now the essential matter to me is the project, and the roof will hold for another couple of years. Could we not leave it that I will try to make something useful happen if you will just sign the papers?

"By the way, have I mentioned that XYZ has offered me a very attractive proposition? It seems that through overhead or fee, or however they do it (I understand that their contracts provide for some amount of "independent" research), they can offer not only better laboratory facilities than I have here at Crossroads, but also quite a satisfactory degree of freedom in my research. Besides, they will permit me to continue to teach one course at Crossroads, if the college so desires. And, naturally, they pay a better wage, with important financial fringe benefits. As I was saying to Mrs. Brown just last night . . ."

We could add to this dissertation some of the obvious points in rebuttal, and both Mr. Smith and Mr. Jones might, for different reasons, accept Professor Brown's little gambit with suggestions regarding his industrial consulting arrangements. But the dissertation has served its purpose as prelude to more sober analysis.

BACKGROUND

The question of proper payment for government sponsored university research has occupied the educational community and federal agencies in a debate running through the past 15 years. Universities have argued that government fiscal policies are unrealistic and inadequate to cover full costs. Sponsoring agencies have been skeptical of university functions which do not bear an obvious relation to the programs they sponsor. Until recently, the number of federal agency policies with respect to university research costs has added confusion to the controversy.

Indirect cost policies are important to universities for a variety of reasons. First, they need the money. Indirect cost payments on government sponsored research contracts and grants are a major item in academic finances. Since these payments are currently running at some $20 million a year for on-campus research, it is clear that any substantial difference between payments and costs amounts to a large sum relative to other university financing.

Second, the total climate for government sponsorship is conditioned by the terms on which universities are paid for services. Scientific relationships and financial relationships may be carried on by separate sets of persons within universities and sponsoring agencies, but the two come close together in the operation of university budgets.

Third, indirect cost payments have an internal influence upon faculty-administrative relationships and upon relationships among departments and faculty members. Being human, faculty engaging in research have some tendency to regard the subtraction of the overhead percentage from their project funds as a subsidy to university administration paid at their expense. Neither can there be a complete absence of feeling that such work is more important to the university than that in fields of less interest to the government. On the other hand, others cannot entirely avoid feeling that the university's general funds flow in disproportionate amount toward the government supported work, not only because of the necessity for covering the gap between actual costs and reimbursement on the research but also in accordance with prestige factors.

No responsible person questions that universities, in their drive to expand research facilities, have made a great contribution to research and education. But there are serious doubts about the effect of the drive in contributing to the precarious financial condition in which many institutions find themselves, and to the fact that the government's position in this process has been anomalous. In encouraging the universities to increase the national output of scientists and engineers, it certainly seems logical to the universities that support of the research which is a part of that training should be designed to ease financing rather than make it hazardous.

The calculation of *direct* costs is almost but not entirely in an equitable state. It is made somewhat complicated by differing university accounting practices, as for example in the charging of employee pension and insurance plans. But it is the *indirect* costs that present as many sets of problems as there are university accounting systems. These are such costs as maintenance, repair and operation of buildings, library services, personnel services, accounting—all of the executive and management operations that do not constitute a direct part of a project. Bookkeeping systems aimed at the outward appearance of conformity, in the area of research, with principles quite different from those governing other university operations are no solution. Neither can universities re-shape their processes of academic accounting to provide a single basis for dealing with the government in the research area. So the problem remains, in its myriad forms, and is alleviated only rather slowly as government and university administrations grow to understand each other better.

Before the federal government became a major source of funds, the research activities of colleges and universities were largely supported by grants-in-aid which assumed that a faculty member was already supported by his institution and which provided the welcome wherewithal to undertake an investigation of his own choosing. Indirect costs were regarded as a contribution by the university to the faculty member's research, giving the university also a desirable stake in the endeavor.

This system worked well as long as the volume of such support was small. It would have continued to work if the financial resources of the universities had increased in proportion to the increase in the volume of their research. But this has not happened. Not only has there been a great increase in research support, especially from public sources, but also the financial resources of educational institutions have been reduced by steady and persistent inflation—all of this in the presence of expanded enrollments.

During World War II many normal university activities were abandoned or substantially decreased so that a large fraction of personnel and space could be devoted to wartime research. The universities were anxious to contribute to the war effort under a policy of "Let's get on with the job and worry about bookkeeping later." At the conclusion of hostilities, however, as it became evident that government sponsored research would become a permanent and enlarged factor if the nation's research capacity was to be expanded, the universities were forced to take a hard look at the costs they were actually incurring and would incur. As a result of conferences between representatives of the War and Navy Departments and business officers of educational institutions, there emerged a plan of cost reimbursement, which came to be known as the "Blue Book" when the document was issued in 1947 for use by those two departments. Its principal provisions were later incorporated in the Armed Services Procurement Regulations, although it was never formally approved by the new Department of Defense or accepted by other federal agencies having such contracts.

THE BLUE BOOK ERA

Numerous questions of interpretation and application arose in connection with audits and administration of contracts, requiring continuing attention. But the procedure was considered generally satisfactory by both universities and sponsoring agencies as a a new way of doing business. However, other federal agencies differed in their attitude and initiated other plans and procedures, some of them distinctly less favorable to universities and consequently the subject of urgent recommendation for change.

Five federal agencies—the Department of Defense; the Atomic Energy Commission; the Department of Health, Education and Welfare; the Department of Agriculture; and the National Science Foundation—have been the principal sponsoring agencies of university research in the past decade. Where the agency was the initiator and the research was obviously of an applied or developmental nature, it was generally agreed that the universities were entitled to recover all costs, both direct and indirect. Differences of opinion began to enter in when the sponsoring agency believed that the educational institution had an equal or greater interest in the research. This led to the continuation of the doctrine of cost participation, carried over from the early days of support from the private foundations—i.e., that the sponsor and grantee should pay jointly for the indirect costs of research. The difference became wide for research in which the university was the instigator—primarily in the field of basic or fundamental research. Beginning, then, with a position that only a small fraction of total direct costs, 15 percent at most, could legitimately be allowed for the indirect costs, attitudes have changed as the operating departments of the federal government have accepted basic research as being vital to their long-term scientific effort.

The National Science Foundation now allows 20 percent for indirect costs which, while on a nationwide average representing probably only about two-thirds of the needed amount, excluding plant amortization, is gratefully accepted by the universities as an interim measure. Only in the case of the National Institutes of Health is the rate now held, by law, to 15 percent.

The significant departure achieved in the 1947 Blue Book was to eliminate the arbitrary assignment of indirect cost allowances on the basis of research definitions or gradation. Its later manifestation, Section 15 of the Armed Services Procurement Regulations, continued the recognition that a mutuality of interests imposed a policy of reasonableness. A key paragraph from the principles appeared as follows:

> In determining the total cost of government research projects, no distinction shall be made between "fundamental" and "applied" research. However, when the government by contract supports a research project of the type which the educational institution might be expected to undertake as a part of its own educational and research program, it may be appropriate for the institution to agree in the contract to sustain part of the cost of the project.

With its recognized shortcomings, the Blue Book nevertheless represented for the first time a unified body of procedure and emphasized a mutual rather than a unilateral determination of indirect costs. In 1955 the National Science Foundation issued a report pointing up the disparity still remaining among agencies of the federal government in the area treated by the Blue Book.* The Foundation made a number of recommendations designed to encourage general acceptance of the Blue Book determination of cost reimbursement procedures, as the Department of Defense appointed a committee to make preliminary studies on its possible revision. In its report, the National Science Foundation took the lead in suggesting that the study be government-wide. The Director of the Bureau of the Budget subsequently, in August, 1956, organized an Interagency Committee of representatives from the several federal agencies having important commitments to university research, with the mission of developing a new set of "Principles" for the Blue Book.

---

* Submitted by the Director, National Science Foundation, to the Director, Bureau of the Budget, June 1955.

The first draft of the Principles, offered to colleges and universities for study in April, 1957, evoked a prompt, vocal reaction that was not at all charmed. In due course, the American Council on Education, the Engineering Colleges Research Council, and the National Federation of College and University Business Officers Association consolidated forces and agreed to work collectively through the American Council, the cement of the consolidation being the impression that the main intent of the new Principles was to move firmly backward. A working group was organized with membership from the three organizations.

During the remainder of 1957 and early in 1958, the Working Group held several meetings with the government's Interagency Committee, in the course of which four redrafts of the proposed Principles were prepared by the Interagency Committee. The Working Group itself presented one complete revision of the document.

On the basis of the final report of the Working Group, the Special Committee on Sponsored Research of the American Council on Education under the chairmanship of President Lee A. DuBridge of the California Institute of Technology, met with the Director of the Bureau of the Budget, in June, 1958. At that meeting it was agreed that there remained at least two fundamental issues concerning, as stated by the representatives of the American Council:

(1) The interrelationship of teaching and research.

(2) The need for alternate methods for allocation of plant operation and maintenance expenses where educational institutions do not maintain space records.

OLD WINE IN NEW BOTTLES

The new Principles were issued as the Bureau of the Budget Circular A-21 on September 10, 1958, designed "to provide to educational institutions recognition of their full allocated costs of research under generally accepted cost accounting principles." The Armed Services Procurement Regulations on November 10, 1958, incorporated the new Circular. To give an idea of the degree of detail that entered into this high-level effort, the primary differences of procedure between A-21 and the former Blue Book are:

(1) A change in the method of allocating the cost of physical plant operation and maintenance from a salary expenditure basis to a use-of-space basis.

(2) Elimination of "student services" cost from allowable general administrative expense, except for that proportion measured by the relationship between hours of work by students and total student hours.

(3) More complete identification and classification of indirect costs as to whether they are allowable or unallowable.

(4) Additions to "allowable costs" of the following items not previously allowed:

    (a) salaries and other office costs of deans of faculty and of graduate schools.

    (b) heads of professional schools, departmental administrative salaries, and other expenses.

(5) Increase in the use charge for library books from $0.04 to $.08 per volume.

The effort made in presenting the government's and universities' points of view was useful and productive in increasing both parties' understanding of indirect costs. Circular A-21 also presents a uniform body of procedure applicable now to most federal agencies and all types of contracts, including grants. This is a boon to the universities in most places where the A-21 formula is employed because the resulting allowances generally fall much closer to actual costs than do any fixed percentages set by law or regulation. Moreover, experience to date indicates that the over-all financial results to universities will probably not be less favorable than under the Blue Book. Finally, the Circular provides for continuing review and possible amendments.

But the university community failed to carry the day in dispelling the notion of university research as a marginal or incremental activity to teaching.

So much for procedures of cost determination. We shall close these remarks with a brief return to the substantive effect of underpayment of research costs at universities where, without regard to absolute size, research financing is large compared with other university financial operations.

A university has an obligation to maintain excellence in intellectual disciplines—some that are currently of interest to federal agencies and others that are not. Modern languages, history, social and behavioral sciences, architecture, earth sciences, literature and philosophy, to name just a few, are all essential areas of scholarly endeavor. They should not be held in check in order to cover the full costs of government sponsored research in the favored fields. On the other hand, desiring to maintain vigorous departments of physics, chemistry, biology and engineering, few universities can keep their faculty in these fields intact without undertaking a substantial volume of government sponsored research, regardless of whether the full costs are covered or not. Private sources of support are generally not available in the amounts required.

Two functions at a university, one covered by sponsored research overhead and the other not, can hardly be in wholly fair competition for inclusion in the university budget of similar items of expense. The allowability of one kind of expense under the government's rules should theoretically (as in practice it does to a degree) make funds available for application equally to other university functions. However, the budget process at a university tends to fall short of the ideal—not entirely unlike the budgets of government. All universities are obligated to conduct their budgeting so that the rich or lean financial treatment they give to their various activities is consistent with the relative importance of these activities according to institutional objectives. And where substantial amounts of sponsored research are at stake, the government should accept its fair share of the obligation, as regards the administrative procedures of reimbursement and, most vital, as regards paying the full cost of the research it sponsors.

To sum up:

(1) The use of a contract to cover government sponsored research lays heavy stress upon the old notion of a bargain between two parties with neither party "giving anything away." In the large volume of research today, a government grant must imply much the same understanding. Mutual respect and understanding can significantly add to or detract from the advantages of government sponsored research at educational institutions.

(2) Public interest requires that government grants and contracts with universities be based upon sound and unassailable cost principles. At the same time, universities are justified in their view that contract coverage of indirect costs recognizes research and teaching as inseparable functions.

(3) The treatment of indirect costs in government sponsored research programs has been strongly influenced by the pre-World War II policies of the private foundations which then properly covered less than the full costs associated with university research. When the amount was small in faculty members and dollar volume, the natural tendency was to treat research as a marginal activity for cost-accounting purposes. The

treatment of research as a by-product of education is both functionally incorrect and financially unrealistic under today's expanded university research programs.

(4) Circular A-21 preserves the notion of "divide and allocate" in the matter of indirect cost coverage. This notion follows naturally from the historical practice mentioned above. In its present form Circular A-21 represents an advance over the old Blue Book but needs careful study in the next few years.

Capital Requirements

The subject is still money. We therefore eavesdrop again on our two friends, Mr. Smith and Mr. Jones, administrators of research, respectively, in government and at Crossroads College.

Mr. Smith: "I must say, Mr. Jones, that I am smarting a bit from your earlier comment about capital write-offs. They stretched the limits of fairness just a little—wouldn't you agree? Of course your facilities are short of what you (and I) would like them to be, but the roof (really, Mr. Jones) is not falling in—nor is the floor collapsing. Besides, in the most important matter of special equipment for Professor Brown's project, surely you will admit that my offer covers current needs down to the last penny. Moreover, under arrangements of previous years, the government has paid the lion's share of the costs of construction of certain other facilities which will support Professor Brown to some extent in this project: for example, your electronic computer and your wind tunnel. Beyond that, as you well know, the government does not duck the issue when really important *new* capital costs are involved in meeting the requirement of our programs. Take your cyclotron built with AEC funds. Or the addition to your biology lab, half of the construction cost of which was borne by a matching grant from the National Institutes of Health. Or your special combustion research chamber, the cost of which you are handling under a rapid amortization scheme which permits you to recover from the government 80% of the initial cost in 10 years.

"As for depreciating your main laboratories against this or any other particular project, Mr. Jones, may I remind you of a practical fact of life: that is, you can't raise facility use payment for one project without raising it for many. And a second practical fact is that there is only so much project money. Each of the dozens of government project officers involved in your program has to make his own project funds go as far as he can—so!—well, Mr. Jones, I think the potential impact not just on Professor Brown but on all of his colleagues will be obvious.

"Now, I know just as well as you that a 2% annual use charge on your laboratory buildings will not replace them in timely fashion, but may I remind you that this practice was born out of university philosophy which has traditionally regarded all but the most obviously temporary of your laboratory buildings as perpetual ornaments rather than as technical facilities having a high obsolescence rate. Besides, give us some credit that we permit you to write off equipment in 15 years.

"But these are details, Mr. Jones, however important they may be separately or in total. The more basic fact is that half of the initial cost of your modern specialized facilities has been, or is being borne by the government, one way or another. You don't want the government to own Crossroads College, do you, Mr. Jones?"

At this point, Mr. Jones is compelled to caution. Seldom indeed is a university research administrator offered such an opportunity (it seems almost contrived) to speak about a subject on which he feels that he could write a book, and would like to—if he could find a publisher having a disregard for sales. He must therefore take great care that his reply is clear and, above all, not exaggerated.

"Mr. Smith," he says, "I want to thank you very much for releasing me from my earlier commitment to avoid philosophy and stick mainly to the current balance sheet. The truth is that you and I cannot find the vitally necessary mutual understanding without looking at how we got to where we are, and at the preconditions of getting to where we must go.

"It is true, as you say, that half of the initial costs of our more specialized new laboratories are borne one way or another by the government. But the other half is on us, and so are our older laboratories—and 80% of the total, old and new, is now devoted to government work.

"The matching grant of NIH enabled our biology addition to be twice as large as we could otherwise have built it. The result is that we do twice as much work for NIH—at a very large percentage deficit because of their 15% limit on the indirect costs—and will run an operating deficit in an amount equal to the building grant in rather short order.

"The combustion research facility is an interesting case study of a different sort. We built it eight years ago on the urging of your predecessor. That's why we were given "rapid" amortization on it: 80% over 10 years. We believed, as your predecessor stated it, that the work to be done represented the wave of the future—the ramjet engine which would in due course largely replace the turbojet in high performance aircraft. Well, Mr. Smith, we have just got the new word which, frankly, we have been expecting for a couple of years. There will be no sponsored research program for the facility next year. The rocket has overtaken the ramjet, and our specialized facility is not adaptable to the quite different technology of rocket combustion research. So we have overtaken ourselves, and have a mostly idle facility a year before the completion of the period of 'rapid' amortization.

"As for our cyclotron, the chassis of which is 10 years old, you may have heard that its future prospects of support are pretty dim unless we undergo a $400,000 modernization program. For this we are offered a matching grant of half the amount, which we shall probably accept. Heigh ho.

"As for your excruciatingly true statement on the internal impact of raising use charges as a means for recovering building costs, I have little to say. The government has strong allies in Professor Brown and his colleagues when a rise in use charge proposed by me seems to them at best a reduction in their project dollars, and possibly a threat to price them out of business. I would, however, add my own obvious remark to yours: that in the end everybody else loses along with Crossroads.

"I could go on, Mr. Smith. Our computer is out of date and only half adequate. Our wind tunnel, at Mach 4, is practically out of business. But, as you say, these are details. Let me take your basic point head-on.

"No, I do not want the government to own Crossroads College. I do believe the government should bear the full cost of necessary, specialized facilities on campuses, regardless of whether they were first proposed by the government or by the university; at today's scales, arguments on the difference between 'solicited' and 'unsolicited' proposals are nonsense. And for laboratories *generally* you should allow not 2 percent but at least 8 percent per year as a use charge for buildings, to which you should add 5 percent of land value, and 15-25 percent of the cost of equipment, depending on its age and obsolescence rate.

"In short, the government should pay its way with regard to the capital which its operations require, just as it should cover the direct and indirect operating costs.

"If you support research as insurance for the future, you must look first to the soundness of the 'insurance industry' on which you depend. In the university segment of that 'industry,' Mr. Smith, the entire community can assure you that your present practices are designed to work against the objective.

"Of course my views are 'parochial,' but that is of no importance.

The objective and the arithmetic are the important things, and they are universal and inexorable."

We can sympathize with Mr. Smith. He probably agrees in large part with Mr. Jones, although he is not likely to make full confession to Mr. Jones in that respect. In any case, as we return to sober dissertation, we may wish for him changes in government policy that will bring him some relief from the Joneses, who are legion.

THE CURRENT NEED

Today, the nation's entire system of higher education is underbuilt and under-equipped.

The President's Science Advisory Committee has recently studied the problem of capital facilities for science and technology in its report (December, 1958) entitled "Strengthening American Science." The Committee referred to the capital deficiencies hampering research within the universities:

> Serious under-investment is handicapping programs in many fields; meteorology and climatology, inorganic chemistry, high temperature research, oceanography, radio astronomy, continental geography, and many of the newer aspects of the life sciences such as microbiology, genetics, the study of growth and the neurological foundations of behavior. In these areas, chosen at random, and in many more, laboratory facilities and instrumentation are required on a wider scale. These are fields in which universities should be doing more research, but financing many of the required facilities is beyond their capacities to provide.

Direct government financing of capital facilities at a university is a relatively new concept. The government's pay-as-you-go philosophy has generally left the universities to provide their own—except where there were none for urgently needed research. Government-owned and university-operated research centers represent one example of such capital outlays. Expensive equipment which has scientific use beyond the scope or life of a particular project is another. Both off-campus and on-campus capital facilities have thus been built in response to a specific need and where no private capital existed. The government has assumed the financing of some kinds of major projects at universities where reactors, accelerators, and computers—and in the biological field, controlled environment facilities—are essential. More recently, a number of interdisciplinary centers for research in materials are being established with federal funds.

The structure of research itself has accelerated the dependence of the universities upon the government for capital funds. While it is still possible to conduct basic research in some areas of science and engineering using small laboratory equipment and inexpensive experimental gear, this is becoming steadily less true. Large-scale computers, particle accelerators for high energy physics, electron microscopes and radio telescopes are a few examples of the expensive capital investments needed to open up new areas of knowledge. The importance of such research is beyond question, but it is difficult to accomplish without government support. Undoubtedly, in fact, more such support will be necessary. However, there are problems, including the need for legislation and special appropriations, the concept of matching grants, and so forth.

An alternative means of assisting with capital facilities is the adoption of policies that would provide greater incentives to educational institutions to finance from their own funds, or even from borrowed funds. During the meeting of the National Research Council in March 1959, much attention was given to the expanding needs for capital facilities at universities. The Council adopted a resolution urging that the government and private sources provide much greater assistance to the financing of such facilities. The President's Science Advisory Committee report also stressed this objective.

The exclusion of interest as a cost, and the limited depreciation allowances for university-financed facilities under research grants and contracts with the government have been major obstacles to the expansion of university research facilities from private sources.

WORKING CAPITAL

Most government sponsored university programs are paid for by a periodic transfer of funds from the sponsoring agency to the educational institution to reimburse for research expenses incurred or to be incurred during the period. On the other hand, university expenditures for salaries, equipment, materials, and services are on a continuing basis as needed. Under this system the inflow and outflow of monies are always in a state of imbalance and require some means of providing working capital and in carrying government accounts receivable. Largely as a carry-over from the government's practice of not recognizing interest as a cost under industrial cost reimbursement contracts, which include a fee for profit, educational institutions are not permitted to recover interest costs in conducting research for federal agencies.

In some instances this interest cost may be considerable. It may be represented by actual borrowing, or it may be financed by advances from endowment funds. In either case it represents a loss which can be severe if the volume of research is large. Failure of federal agencies to make prompt payment can burden an institution to the extent that many have found it profitable to maintain special staffs to expedite the payment procedure. Government budget dynamics being what they are, institutions are sometimes embarrassed by the accumulation of unpaid federal obligations at the end of the government fiscal year. One writer has noted a recent case of an institution which advanced $2.5 million from its endowment funds in order to pay its research bills after an accumulation of delayed payments from federal agencies.*

The variety of practices followed by sponsoring agencies further complicates this problem and has fostered special relationships solely in the matter of payment. Each agency is organized somewhat differently in the conduct of its financial affairs and in the inter-relation of its financial, contracting, and technical sections. Knowledge of the financial structure of sponsoring agencies is essential to the efficient conduct of research on a campus.

The problem of interest is not easy, because of the legal restrictions against interest and of the limited working capital in the hands of educational institutions. If a way could be found to change existing legislation, the universities would view this form of relief enthusiastically. However, the tying up of working capital can be, and is with some universities, reduced through special advance payment procedures.† These can be arranged so as to finance fully both grants and contracts for research as well as facilities construction. They can be arranged on an individual contract basis or, if the volume of research warrants, under a master pool agreement to finance all contracts of a given institution with a federal agency.

In recent years the federal agencies sponsoring the largest volume of university research have developed effective payment procedures. Some agencies newer to such sponsorship, or whose volume is small, have lagged in developing this area along with their university counterparts.

USE CHARGES FOR EQUIPMENT AND FACILITIES

Raymond J. Woodrow of Princeton University has pointed to inconsistencies in the federal government's present treatment of interest cost

---

* Lloyd Morey, "Review of Circular A-21, Bureau of the Budget, for the Comptroller, Department of Defense," March 19, 1959.

† Advance payments are provided under certain conditions as authorized by Appendix E of the Armed Services Procurement Regulations.

and depreciation rates.* Mr. Woodrow uses the example of a large computer facility employed in government-sponsored research. If the university rents a computer, it can charge the full rent against research grants and contracts on an allocated basis. The rent paid to the company furnishing the computer includes a more rapid depreciation than the university itself could obtain, and also includes a profit which compensates the company not only for the funds invested but, in addition, quite properly, for the business risks. On the other hand, if the institution buys the computer it will obtain a lower allowance for depreciation and no recognition whatsoever of the income which might have been realized from the funds advanced to purchase the computer.

Mr. Woodrow further cites the disparity between the use charges which a university can make on its own capital facilities in government sponsored research and those which it must make if government owned facilities are put to use in research projects sponsored by private sources. If the latter were allowed for all facilities connected with government research grants and contracts, there seems little doubt that more facilities would be financed by the institutions themselves.

EXPLOSIVE GROWTH

Since 1945, science and technology have pushed to the center of national attention with an urgency that no previous Congress or President could have dreamed of. The spectacular accomplishments of university people in the physical sciences and in engineering have been accompanied by equally spectacular growth in the capital required for their research.

The field of particle accelerators is a good case in point. As late as 1930 the idea of a cyclotron was first reported in the magazine *Science* by Professor Ernest O. Lawrence of the University of California.

Professor M. S. Livingston traces the development of particle accelerators from this early work at the University of California and at the Cavendish Laboratory of Cambridge University.† Professor Livingston cites four waves of development which have dominated the particle accelerator field, based on different concepts of acceleration and focusing.

> As each type of machine was rapidly developed to approach
> its theoretical energy ceiling, another principle came along

---

* Raymond J. Woodrow, "Encouraging University Expenditures on Capital Facilities for Science," Princeton, New Jersey, March 31, 1959.

† M. S. Livingston, "Early Development of Particle Accelerators," *American Journal of Physics*, Vol. 27, No. 9, pages 626-629, December, 1959.

to provide a new step upward in energy. The voltage multiplier, the cyclotron, the betatron, synchrocyclotron, electron synchrotron, and proton synchrotron have each in turn held the voltage record temporarily.

In the short span of 28 years the energy levels achieved by the various machines has risen from 80,000 electron volts to the energy range of the large modern accelerators which range from 100 million electron volts to 10,000 million electron volts (10 Bev). The CERN Laboratory in Geneva (European Organization for Nuclear Research) has a new proton alternating gradient synchrotron which operates at 29 Bev energy. Construction is underway at Brookhaven National Laboratory for a similar machine rated between 25 and 30 Bev. In Cambridge, Massachusetts, the largest electron synchrotron yet conceived is being constructed as a joint Harvard University-M.I.T. facility, under the sponsorship of the Atomic Energy Commission. This machine will produce energies up to 6 Bev.

Professor Livingston graphically illustrates these dramatic increases in energies achieved with the several accelerator types by plotting energy on a logarithmic scale against time (see Chart III).

The envelope of the curves which indicate the development of the various types of accelerators is found to be close to a straight line, indicating an increase of energy by a factor of ten every six years! The progress of individual accelerator types is shown by the numbered curves below the linear envelope, which gives the reader some idea of the relative order of the various accelerators on the energy scale.

A proposed electron linear accelerator at Stanford University, estimated to cost in excess of $100 million, is expected to develop energies up to 50 Bev. Designs are started in the USSR for an accelerator rated at 50 Bev.

Clearly, no single university, or even group of universities acting jointly could hope to finance these large undertakings in the physical sciences. No one seriously questions this conclusion. The funds involved are so large that special acts of Congress and special appropriations within the departments of government are required so that the operating budgets of sponsoring agencies will not be taxed unduly. The field of high energy physics in particular is acknowledged to be closely related to the national interest and perhaps survival.

The debate over capital facilities for universities begins to form when the capital outlay is for research in which the government's role is thought to be that of providing aid to research rather than supporting research urgently needed for national purposes. This distinction is often

CHART III

GROWTH IN ENERGY LEVELS OF
PARTICLE ACCELERATORS, 1930–1960

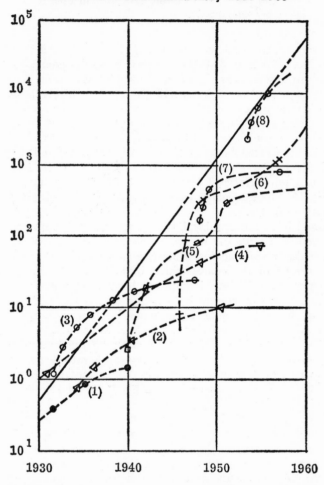

(1) D. C. Generators   (5) Betatron

(2) Electrostatic Gen.   (6) Electron Synchrotron

(3) Cyclotron   (7) Synchro-Cyclotron

(4) Proton Linear   (8) Proton Synchrotron

referred to as the difference between *supported* research and *purchased* research. It is the same distinction that has contributed so much confusion to the controversy over the proper share of university indirect costs that government sponsored research projects should bear.

MEETING THE NEED

When the federal government provides the capital costs for research the university would cover if it had the money, it might appear that a proper university cost has been shifted to the federal taxpayer. If one looks at the total research activity of all universities in relation to the objectives of all federal agencies, however, the situation is quite different.

Charles V. Kidd has stated the difficulty of working with this distinction:

> The sum total of all federal programs for support of research in universities can be considered a declaration of national objectives and an expression of national policy. This policy is made particularly clear by the willingness of Congress to appropriate funds for the support of university research which has no immediate relevance to the operating tasks of the federal agencies and to provide funds to expand the nation's research resources. Participation in this national effort involves many universities in uncongenial large-scale research, and it creates new academic and financial difficulties for them. The total effect of the federal activities is not entirely to help the universities do more of what they wish to do, but to involve them in the achievement of national goals which they did not set. This involvement can come about for a university as a whole even though the effect of the federal funds on individual faculty members is to help them do precisely what they want to do.
>
> It is not valid to argue that the national interest, expressed as the operating need of a federal agency, is served when research is purchased, but that the national interest, expressed as furtherance of free research with no necessary relevance to the operating needs of federal agencies, is not served when research is supported. Equally significant national needs are met through the two different types of financing. Faculty members whose free research is supported serve the interest of the nation as surely and perhaps more importantly than when they undertake contract research at the urging of a federal agency.*

---

* Charles V. Kidd, *American Universities and Federal Research,* Harvard University Press, 1959, pp. 86 and 87.

The question at issue is not whether the government should provide capital for higher education. That was settled in the affirmative with the enactment of the Morrill Act of 1862 and has not been seriously debated since. The question rather, in sponsored research, is how best to provide the funds—in the interests of both the government and the universities.

All institutional criteria which apply to the placement of research problems in an academic setting are magnified when large capital investments are involved. For one reason, the financial risks can be great for the university. For another, the choice of facilities that will enhance the development of the institution along desired lines must be made in a state of imperfect knowledge about future scientific developments in a particular field, as well as uncertainty about the future interest of university investigators. Clearly, in spite of the delicate guesswork, there is a high premium on making sound judgments. The commitment of capital funds affects not only the future pattern of research at an institution and the professional development of its faculty but also the training and education of future students.

The limited funding practices of the federal government make it difficult for an agency to enter into long-term commitments for capital facilities. These limitations add to the financial risks of universities when they underwrite the cost of specialized buildings and equipment with their own funds on the assumption that government agencies will amortize a large part of the capital expenditures. Some university facilities have been constructed on "expressions of intent" that failed to materialize, because of either a shift in the research focus of sponsoring agencies or changes in their amortization practices. One undesirable effect of these restrictions is the possibility that in order to recover their original investment, universities may be led artificially to favor particular research interests.

In spite of the difficulties, however, the provision of capital facilities by federal agencies has resulted in widespread improvements in university research. Their effect is often to foster growth in areas of latent potential. To take a few examples, the construction of large particle accelerators, wind tunnels, magnets, ultracentrifuges, digital and analog computation facilities and spectrographic laboratories have stimulated universities to make basic contributions in such important areas as high energy physics, aerodynamics, materials, molecular biology, automation and organic chemistry.

At a national level it would be difficult to establish meaningful correlation between the *amount* of government support and the potential loss of freedom in a particular field. To illustrate this point, we need only note the contrast in the proportion of support provided by the federal government in several major fields: Of all university research in physics, 96 percent is financed by federal agencies. The corresponding figure for the life sciences is 50 percent, and for the social sciences 25 percent. To quote one observer:

> It would be difficult to present a persuasive argument to the effect that postwar research in physics in this country is more controlled by the federal government, or less productive, or of a lower intellectual caliber, or more threatened with federal restrictions, than is research in the life sciences or the social sciences. The problem is not answered by reiterating that "he who pays the piper calls the tune." *

The truth is that universities have inadequate funds of their own to invest in research and must rely on factors other than funds to retain control over their research programs. Along with periodic appeals to private sources of capital, these "other" means include the adoption and enforcement of sound policies, an uncompromising insistence upon high intellectual standards, and insistence upon government capital funds under satisfactory terms and conditions. In conclusion, the recommendations of the President's Science Advisory Committee suggest a useful point of departure in the matter of research capital for the universities. The following statements appear in their report, *Strengthening American Science:*

> (1) In its support of science and technology, the government should recognize that adequate capital support is a necessary part of research and make provision for meeting the capital needs of the programs it supports.

> (2) The Federal Council for Science and Technology should prepare a projection of the capital requirements planned by federal agencies to meet their scientific and technological needs and provide a set of priorities.

> (3) In making grants and contracts, government agencies should provide, as an element of cost, for new instruments and facilities as well as continuous modernization of older equipment used by universities and non-profit institutions.

> (4) Those government departments and agencies concerned should uniformly modify their grant and contract provisions to permit universities and non-profit research institutions to

---

* Charles V. Kidd, *American Universities and Federal Research*, page 91.

charge the full cost of research performed for the government —including overhead—and to amortize capital expenditures as an allowable cost.

University Participation in Government Policy Making

The United States emerged from World War II with unexpectedly large responsibilities for world leadership. We also faced a revolution in science and technology more profound in its implications than we were prepared to cope with in any deliberate fashion.

The spectacular achievements of science and engineering during World War II convinced government officials and legislators that these fields would have far reaching social, economic, and international consequences. Dr. Vannevar Bush's *Science, the Endless Frontier,* written in 1945, and the five-volume study, *Science and Public Policy* by the President's Scientific Research Board in 1947 urged that science be looked upon as a major national resource. Many others joined the chorus, and research in the physical and engineering sciences did indeed receive government support which, while considerably less than today, was unprecedented in peacetime. But, most of all, it was the continuing truculence and rapid rise of the Soviet Union that led to the conviction that science is not only broadly important for its own sake but vital to the national security, of which prestige is an important part. During the year after the Communist invasion of South Korea, federal obligations for research and development rose by 60 percent, remaining in the new high area until they took still another large jump following the first Sputnik.

These added sums were distributed with judgment on where the money would be most productive in advancing the government's objectives in science and technology, as nearly as these could be determined. Universities of course shared proportionately with other claimants. There was a corollary, however, to the increased spending that had a second, and in a sense disproportionate, effect on universities. That was the intensified call on academic institutions and individuals as advisors in government decisions, regarding science and education principally, but going beyond that to the application of scientific knowledge and method to a wide range of government policy questions, especially in fields related to the national security. Since much of the nation's intellectual capacity is concentrated in the universities, it was natural that the university scientists and the universities themselves should become prominently involved in the postwar governmental hierarchy through participation in innumerable committees, boards, panels, and study groups as well as in permanent organizations established to provide specialized knowledge on a continuing basis.

Don K. Price describes the growth of the government's "machinery of advice" as a coalescence of three major lines—the use of part-time committees, the resort to special study contracts, and the evolution of a system of operations research, to provide continuing advice. Whereas standing advisory committees serving on a part-time basis were a familiar administrative device, the employment of scientists outside government under special study contracts, and in permanent organizations for continuing advice, was entirely a postwar phenomenon. In atomic energy and national defense, in particular, elaborate structures were formed to enlist the scientific community in the exercise of executive authority. In both fields the need to make major decisions based on objective and expert knowledge led to major innovations in government decision processes. In short, as Mr. Price puts it:

> The United States is the only nation that has ever been willing to support and create private institutions to make studies on problems combining scientific and military considerations —problems of a sort that would elsewhere be considered the very heart of general staff planning. The private institutions that are now largely supported by military funds are the most important sources of independent, skeptical, and uninhibited criticism of military thinking.*

Today, each of the military services and the Joint Chiefs of Staff are served separately by private organizations whose functions are to bring a wide range of scientific knowledge to bear upon military operations and weapons systems development. The RAND Corporation, a non-profit enterprise with headquarters in Santa Monica, California, serves the Air Force; the Operations Research Office, a subsidiary of the Johns Hopkins University, serves the Army as does the Human Resources Office at George Washington University; the Operations Evaluation Group, located in the Office of the Chief of Naval Operations is directed and staffed by the Massachusetts Institute of Technology; the Institute for Defense Analyses, a non-profit association of universities, manages the scientific organization supporting the Weapons Systems Evaluation Group which serves the Joint Chiefs of Staff. More recently, the Mitre Corporation has been organized with M.I.T. support, at the request of the Department of Defense, to provide systems

---

* Don K. Price, *Government and Science,* New York University Press, 1954, pp. 143, 144.

analysis and engineering services for air defense and other major new communications systems. The participation of university personnel in these and other enterprises has thus become critical to our national defense and survival.

Universities have also participated in government decision-making by administering study groups. These provide advice on broad strategic problems which require an interplay of scientific, technical and political considerations. The Atomic Energy Commission and the Department of Defense have made especially heavy use of the university study groups—for example the Lexington Study to investigate nuclear powered flight, Project Charles dealing with continental air defense, Project East River to advise on civil defense, the Hartwell Project to study sea transport during wartime, and Project Vista to examine tactics and strategy for certain conditions of large-scale war. These studies have implicated faculty members and universities in decisions of great national consequence. They represent an important means by which the government has augmented its scientific resources.

The use of the universities to organize and manage some government oriented establishments is a postwar phenomenon that has levied its price upon universities. Their strong attraction for intellectual manpower, their relative freedom of action with regard to personnel policies, and their integrity in matters of public trust have all drawn attention to the universities as a fertile environment for creating new organizations.

The responsibilities of organizing and managing these new ventures place a heavy burden upon high-ranking university administrators and correspondingly reduce the amount of time for the discharge of traditional university functions.*

Where the advice of scientific bodies under university management enters into decisions of great public interest, the universities have in some instances sought the protection afforded by numbers, as in the case of the Institute for Defense Analyses.

Heavy reliance is placed also upon individual faculty members and university administrators in part-time advisory committees. Charles V. Kidd estimates that the total number of persons serving on such committees is probably well over 1,000, with more than half from the educational community.

Within the White House, the President's Science Advisory Committee,

---

* For a thoughtful and entertaining essay on the demanding responsibilities of academic administration, see the article by President Douglas Knight of Lawrence College, "The Waking Nightmare: Or How Did I Get Into This?", Association of American Colleges Bulletin, December 1958.

during the first eighteen months following Sputnik I, utilized the part-time services of 160 scientists and engineers from industry, education, and government. These consultants served on twenty-seven *ad hoc* panels which completed thirty-seven major studies and reports, about half of which dealt with ways through which science and engineering can serve national security objectives.*

Finally, there is the considerable number of university members who serve full time on leave of absence in government posts.

Beyond the contribution of public service, which is owed to government, it is fair to note that the universities benefit to a considerable extent for such loan of their skills. By filling government posts and serving advisory committees they help attune government to the needs, potentials, and realities of education and university research. We have noted that their success in influencing the scientific directions and content of government programs, especially in basic research, has not been matched in areas of management vital to them. It may seem to some on occasion that university advisors form such swarms in Washington as to obscure the sun, influencing executives and legislators out of proportion to their practical knowledge. But it remains the case that in a matter of closest personal interest to so many of them—as, for example, the stability of financial support in campus laboratories—the average researcher back home in June of any year, when the matter of his next-year commitments are at a painful peak, is from half certain to highly uncertain about what the new government fiscal year will bring. And, quite seriously, the unnecessary fret is a significant national waste.

Nevertheless, the associations fostered by university participation in advisory committees contribute to greater understanding and mutual respect, which in the end must form the basis of effective cooperation between government and the educational community.

Strengthening American Science and Engineering

Of our approximately 1,900 colleges and universities, only a third offer graduate degrees. Fewer than 10 percent award the doctorate. In fields of research of special interest to the federal government, graduate education is highly concentrated. For example, 15 universities award half the doctorates in physics; 10 account for half the doctorates in engineering. Eleven offer half the doctorates in mathematics. Nor is

---

* "Capsule Conclusions," speech by J. R. Killian, Jr., Special Assistant to the President for Science and Technology, Symposium on Basic Research, New York City, May 14, 1959.

the pattern different in the life sciences; for example, a third of all graduate degrees in biochemistry are granted by four universities.

Graduate schools stand at the very pinnacle of our system. They play a decisive role in setting the pattern of excellence. In research they play a major role in setting much of the scientific and technological pace at which our society advances.

Federal funds for university research flow toward the strong graduate centers, for there is where research strength also resides. (This concentration is reflected in Table 2.) The base is being broadened, as is must be, in the deepest sense of the interest of our society. In the past half dozen years the number of universities qualifying for federal research grants and contracts has increased by more than a third, to approximately 250. Of course some of this expansion represents an investment of "venture capital" by government, an expression more of confidence in the future than of recognition of established excellence. On the other hand, government does not unerringly find all resources in research which are deserving of nourishment. But the trend is encouraging.

TABLE 2*

DISTRIBUTION OF FEDERAL RESEARCH FUNDS AMONG UNIVERSITIES, 1953-54

University Grouping According to Volume of Research Grants and Contracts	Number of Institutions	Average Number of Grants and Contracts per Institution	Total in Each Group (Millions of Dollars)	Group Percent	Cumulative Percent
All Institutions	173	45	$141.6	100%	0%
$5 million and above	6	258	47.3	33	33
$3-$5	8	193	31.4	22	55
$1-$3	22	84	36.2	26	81
$0.5-$1	18	66	12.7	9	90
$0.25-$0.5	18	37	6.5	5	95
$0.1-$0.25	32	20	5.2	4	99
Under $0.1	69	5	2.3	1	100

Source: NSF, *Scientific Activities for Research and Development in Colleges and Universities—Expenditures and Manpower, 1953-1954,* Washington: GPO, 1959.
 * Does not include funds for research centers managed by educational institutions.

The inherent disciplines which require the government science administrator to be able to defend the professional worthiness of the recipients of his bounty give reasonable assurance that expression reflects a genuine expansion of competence and not just his zeal for democracy. Indeed, as the less strong are helped, the first essential is a larger output, from the existing centers of strength, of trained research supervisors. The system therefore demands that in broadening the base the strong also be made stronger—with the government, representing all the people, winning both ways.

Some 70% of all university research is currently sponsored by the federal government. The funds are in the main provided by five agencies —the Department of Defense; the Department of Health, Education and Welfare; the Atomic Energy Commission; the National Science Foundation; and the Department of Agriculture. Together these five obligated over 96 percent of the total federal funds for on-campus research during fiscal 1959, not including operating monies for the research centers managed by the colleges and universities. Table 3 sets forth the sources of these funds for fiscal year 1959. The National Aeronautics and Space Administration is a relative newcomer to the roster of federal agencies having substantial research programs within the educational community. NASA's predecessor, the National Advisory Committee on Aeronautics, conducted research on a much smaller scale with less resort to university resources.

TABLE 3

FEDERAL OBLIGATIONS FOR RESEARCH & DEVELOPMENT AT EDUCATIONAL INSTITUTIONS, FISCAL 1959
(Dollar Figures in Millions)

	Educational Institutions Proper		Research Centers Managed by Universities	
1. Department of Defense	$124	32.4%	$ 97	32.0%
2. Department of Health, Education and Welfare	111	29.0	—	—
3. Atomic Energy Commission	57	14.8	186	61.1%
4. National Science Foundation	46	12.0	—	—
5. Department of Agriculture	31	8.1	—	—
6. National Aeronautics and Space Administration	8	2.1	20	6.9
7. All other Agencies	5	1.6	—	—
	$383	100.0%	$303	100.0%

Source: National Science Foundation, *Federal Funds for Science, VIII,* Washington: GPO, 1960.

Note: Dollar amounts do not add correctly because of rounding.

Although there is talk about the critical importance of basic research, it must be recognized that the federal agencies remain principally committed to development as opposed to research. Of total federal obligations of $7.2 billion for research and development in fiscal 1959, 77 percent was allocated to development, 16 percent for applied research, and less than 7 percent was for basic research.

Table 4 shows the breakdown of these various categories, according to the research and development obligations of each agency. The Department of Defense which provides the largest amount for research in the colleges and universities, placed 2.1 percent of its total R&D budget in basic research in contrast to 85.8 percent for development purposes. The comparable figures for the Atomic Energy Commission, the second largest federal source of research support in the universities, were 12.4 per cent and 77 per cent.

TABLE 4

FEDERAL OBLIGATIONS FOR RESEARCH & DEVELOPMENT, FISCAL 1959

(Dollar Figures in Millions)

	Percent of Own R&D Budget for Basic Research	Percent of Own R&D Budget for Applied Research	R&D Budget for Development Percent of Own	Total R&D
1. National Science Foundation	100.0%	(none)%	(none)%	$ 57
2. Department of Health, Education and Welfare	30.0	68.2	1.8	224
3. National Aeronautics and Space Agency	29.7	24.3	46.0	303
4. Department of Interior	27.9	53.2	19.9	62
5. Department of Commerce	23.7	42.6	33.7	28
6. Department of Agriculture	23.0	72.8	4.2	119
7. Atomic Energy Commission	12.4	10.6	77.0	773
8. Department of Defense	2.1	12.1	85.8	5,581
9. Federal Aviation Agency	(none)	1.8	98.2	28
	6.7%	16.0%	77.3%	$7,234

Source: Derived from National Science Foundation, *Federal Funds for Science, VIII,* Washington: Government Printing Office, 1960.

Note: Total is not exact because of some $36.8 million R&D funds of several other agencies.

It is this orientation of federal funds toward development that leads to continuing caution in universities enjoying federal sponsorship that they not be diverted from basic university objectives. The question is not whether they have yielded to undesirable influences but rather to what extent they can succeed, with federal support, in meeting their enlarged responsibilities and opportunities at a time when university goals are rising rapidly in the values of advanced societies. Qualitatively, those universities which have insisted upon rigorous standards of excellence have also gained most from federal funds. As Charles V. Kidd puts it in *American Universities and Federal Research:*

> The most significant factor affecting university research programs has not been the federal government but the standards of excellence and discrimination maintained by the intangible social pressures of the faculty. The most important effect of the federal funds has therefore been to provide momentum in directions set by cultural values and by forces within universities.

THE GAPS

The present interest of federal agencies in university research produces a concentration of funds in three major fields—life sciences, physical sciences, and engineering. Over 96 percent of the $1.4 billion obligated for research (not including development) by the federal government in fiscal 1959 was for studies in these three major fields, both within and outside the educational community. Detailed information on the breakdown of this support within education is not available at this writing. However, the proportions shown in Table 5 for the fiscal year 1953-54 give an indication of the heavy weighting of funds.

During fiscal 1953-54, for example, the federal government sponsored 96 percent of total university research in the physical sciences, 50 percent in the life sciences and 83 percent in the branches of engineering.

These impressive percentages belie the fact that there are significant gaps within each of the three major fields sponsored heavily by federal funds. Engineering is a good example. In a recent study, the Engineering College Research Council estimated that almost 25 per cent of the nation's proved research capacity in engineering schools was idle in 1956-57 for lack of funds.

This estimate was based on the amount of time the faculties of 108 engineering schools could have spent on more research without interfering with teaching, committed research, committee assignments, and

TABLE 5

SPONSORSHIP OF UNIVERSITY RESEARCH 1953-54
(Millions of Dollars)

Field	Government	Universities	Other	Total
Life Sciences	$ 34	$ 7.6	$25.3	$ 66
Physical Sciences	47	2.5	5.5	56
Engineering	52	3.4	7.8	63
Psychology	5	0.6	0.9	7
Social Sciences	3	3.0	6.2	12
All Others	1	0.4	0.6	2
	$142	$17.5	$46.3	$206

Source: National Science Foundation, *Scientific Activities for Research and Development in Colleges and Universities—Expenditures and Manpower, 1953-54.* Washington: GPO 159.

other responsibilities. Only 10 percent of the institutions in the study answered *no* to the question of whether any excess research capacity was available on their campuses; the remaining 90 percent answered *yes* in varying amounts. In the Council's words:

> The areas of engineering science which appear to be most in need of intensive basic research are metallurgy (high and low temperature), ceramics (ceramics, coatings, etc.), aeronautics (shock tubes, wind tunnels, etc.), civil engineering (water and waste treatment), isotopes, heat transfer, servomechanisms, and high-speed computors. More could be named.
>
> In an age of rapid technological advancements there will always be a strong demand for more knowledge, especially basic knowledge. Though they are ready and willing to contribute, our schools may not be able to act without substantial financial assistance.*

What is true of engineering is also true of the life sciences and the physical sciences. These gaps in coverage within the better-supported fields point up the difficulties of finding suitable ways to finance the less supported fields, notably the social sciences and the humanities. The need for increased understanding in these fields has been heightened by the same forces that have prompted the explosive rise in federal spending for research in the physical sciences and engineering. Recently,

---

* Engineering Colleges Research Council, "A Survey of Research in the Nation's Engineering Colleges, Capabilities and Potentialities, July 1956-July 1957," published in June 1958.

encouraging developments have strengthened the standing of the social sciences in the federal government. In particular, their increased recognition by the National Science Foundation and the White House is encouraging. Within the past year, NSF has roughly doubled its support of the social sciences, and although the amount is still small, the direction and rate of change are significant.

EPILOGUE

The federal government is clearly committed to a dominant role in stimulating, promoting, and supporting scientific progress in the United States. More than ever before, the nation's strength in science and engineering resides in the quality and resiliency of our educational system, in these specialized fields and a host of others. During the past twenty years, the universities and the federal government have entered upon a course that has been responsible for significant changes in our society. There is good reason to believe these changes will continue and accelerate in the decade ahead.

In seeking to strengthen our university resources for the challenges and opportunities of this scientific age, greater public recognition, understanding, and appreciation of intellectual pursuits are prime requisites. As the great English mathematician and philosopher Alfred North Whitehead put it in 1916:

> In the conditions of modern life the rule is absolute. The race which does not value trained intelligence is doomed. Not all your heroism, not all your social charm, not all your wit, not all your victories on land or at sea, can move back the finger of fate. Today we maintain ourselves. Tomorrow science will have moved forward yet another step, and there will be no appeal from the judgment which will then be pronounced on the uneducated.

Acknowledgment

In preparing this discussion the authors were helped in many ways by their M.I.T. colleagues, to whom a large debt is owed. We have purposely not identified their individual contributions. Doing so would have unduly burdened the document and might have conveyed the impression that our observations are overly based upon M.I.T.'s experience—whereas in fact, we have attempted to reflect as adequately as we could the experience of the educational community generally.

4.

Issues in federal aid to higher education

Why Consider Federal Aid?

✦ JOHN A. PERKINS

✦ DANIEL W. WOOD

R ecently the federal government has moved far upstage in the unfolding drama of higher education's future. The prime reason is financial. The well-publicized and inevitable growth in collegiate enrollments comes at a time when resources are already too limited for present responsibilities. Inflation and modest expansion have reduced the significance of endowments in collegiate income. War-induced federal taxation has reacted adversely upon large private benefactions of the Rockefeller, Vanderbilt, and Carnegie variety. At the same time resentment of high federal taxes has generated resistance against heavier levies by the states and municipalities which traditionally have been the chief source of support of public higher education.

140

◆ JOHN A. PERKINS, president of the University of Delaware and former Under Secretary of Health, Education and Welfare, is an authority on federal, state, and local government. In 1945 he was assistant director for training of the International City Managers Association. Later he was budget director of the State of Michigan, with over-all responsibilities for about 100 state agencies, and a member of the State Planning Commission. In 1948-49 he was state controller. Dr. Perkins was president of the American Society for Public Administration in 1953-54. He has also been on the executive board of UNESCO. In 1955 he was on a governor's committee to study the needs and problems of schools and colleges in Delaware, and in addition, has served on the joint committee on Voluntary Gifts to Public Colleges and Universities. Dr. Perkins is the author of two books and of more than fifty articles in professional journals.

◆ DANIEL W. WOOD, administrative assistant to the president of the University of Delaware, has written numerous articles on problems in education. Mr. Wood is a member of the Association for Higher Education, the Delaware State Education Association and a delegate to the Southern Regional Education Board. He is a former teacher in the School of Education of the University of Delaware.

While educators have found larger revenues difficult to obtain, the inadequacies of collegiate budgets have been spotlighted by rising prices in both operation and in the construction of new buildings. The faculty shortage reflects the low birth rate of the Great Depression years. But, especially in science and engineering, it has been aggravated by economic prosperity and society's, especially industry's, sudden appreciation of the need for men with the doctor's degree. Business can pay the new Ph.D. better than the university can pay the average professor who readied him for scientific employment. The inadequate standard of living reflected by current college and university budgets constitutes a grim background. Against it the financial problems caused by an approximate doubling of the number of students enrolled in higher education must be considered.

141

HEAVY ENROLLMENT INCREASES ANTICIPATED

Within a decade the college-age group will be greater than the total population of the United States a century ago. There are two reasons for this growth. First, in recent years there have been enough children born each year to populate a city more than twice the size of Los Angeles. The oldest of these were born long enough ago to approach college next year. (Some educators would go too far in limiting enrollments to an intellectual elite. There is no genetic evidence that youth born in the past 20 years has college-level intelligence in any less proportion than present and past college-age groups.) The rising tide of students, however, will vary from one state to another. For example, the birth rate since 1940 has jumped in Oklahoma by only 17 percent; in Florida by 272 percent.

The second reason for the unprecedented increase in college enrollments is that the percentage of young people of college age continuing their education beyond high school increases about one percent each year. Whereas, in the 1930's less than 15 percent of this age group actually enrolled, today more than 30 percent seek education of true collegiate quality. It is inconceivable that *all* young people will eventually come to expect this education; yet, predictions are frequent that 50 percent will do so. This will be the case especially if a proportionate share of young women with ability decide to seek the baccalaureate degree. Because of tradition and opportunity, there will also be variations among the states in the proportion of young people going to college. For example, in Utah more than 40 percent of the college-age population already attend. In states where less than the average proportion of young people now go to college, a big percentage jump, as well as the effect of the birth rate, must be anticipated. Furthermore, there is not necessarily any positive correlation between the likely increases in collegiate enrollment and the financial resources of a geographic area.

WHOSE RESPONSIBILITY—PUBLIC OR PRIVATE HIGHER EDUCATION?

Important to any consideration of financing enrollment increases in American colleges is whether private or public institutions are likely to accommodate the bulk of the students. The past may foretell the future. At the turn of the century 72 percent of the students were in private colleges. In 1958-59, almost 60 percent were in public ones and 61 percent of the freshmen entered them. Moreover, the trend toward public institutions has accelerated in the present decade. There are several reasons for this shift: the great public universities have developed branches and evening extension and graduate programs. Public junior colleges have increased in number and one-time teachers' colleges have expanded in breadth and stature. To what extent the private colleges will expand or new ones evolve is difficult to predict. The advantages of growth to the college now too small are sometimes overlooked. With fewer than 1,000 students, it is difficult to offer a rich curriculum with adequate instructional and living facilities along with complete testing and guidance services at anything like a reasonable cost per student. In 1956, however, 20 percent of our colleges had enrollments of fewer than 200, 29 percent 200 to 500 and 22 percent from 500 to 999. Seventy-one percent of our colleges had enrollments of fewer than 1,000. Still, expectations generally are that there will be an ever-greater reliance upon public programs of higher education. The reason is that the ultimate distribution of students between public and private higher learning doubtless will be determined by the likely pattern of financial support. For example, one prediction is that unless the fees are raised substantially in public higher education, 80 percent of all college students will be enrolled in it. The hundreds of small colleges, most of them private, need to expand; but whether or not they can do so, depends upon their finding money for expansion.

THE RAPID GROWTH OF KNOWLEDGE

Another reason why higher education will require additional funds has been often overlooked. The mushroom-like growth of knowledge in recent decades requires that our colleges and universities offer instruction in areas of knowledge which were virtually non-existent 20 years ago: electronics, oceanography, X-ray spectroscopy, geophysics, biophysics, astrophysics, microbiology, radio astronomy, group dynamics, and the heretofore neglected rare languages. Instruction in these fields requires an ever-increasing number of new faculty specialists and new and expensive equipment such as electronic computers, radio telescopes, electron microscopes, hydrogen fusion devices, and X-ray spectrographs, not to mention new books for libraries. Most of these requirements transcend the financial means of most colleges and even universities. They must be available, however, if students are to be educated in a late twentieth century manner. Furthermore, the most expensive aspect of all higher education, the graduate professional schools, such as those in medicine and dentistry, must be expanded in number, as must doctoral programs in such fields as physics and chemical engineering. To maintain the present ratio of medical doctors per thousand of population, it has been estimated a new medical school must be established each year for the next two decades. In all probability these will be public ones attached to public universities.

FINANCIAL REQUIREMENTS BY 1970

Wherever the additional students are to be educated and new programs offered, and however the institutions to accommodate them all are to be sponsored, a great deal more money will be needed. Estimates vary as to the precise amount required annually for operations by 1970, from a low of $9½ billion to a high of $13 billion. Current expenditures for higher education come to about $3.5 billion. This means that from $6 to $9 billion in new money is needed by 1970. Projected evenly by years, this comes to a minimum of $600 million in new funds annually simply for current operation. The American Council on Education and the United States Office of Education have estimated the magnitude of higher education's capital expansion needs in the next decade. The first agency predicts a $15 billion requirement; the second a $33 billion outlay. The big question obviously is where new money of the order required for both operations and capital growth ($21 to $40 billion) can be found and channeled into higher education with reasonable effort.

Where Can the Money Come From?

First, a look at where higher education's funds have come from in the past. Generally, there are four major sources of collegiate income: (1) governments, (2) students, (3) gifts, and (4) endowments. The proportion of income from these several sources varies greatly between privately endowed and publicly-supported institutions:

ESTIMATED SOURCES OF EDUCATIONAL AND GENERAL
INCOME FROM 1,937 INSTITUTIONS*

1957-1958

	All institutions	669 Public Institutions	1,268 Private Institutions
Tuition and Fees	25.3%	7.9%	46.3%
Governments	48.9%	77.5%	14.6%
Gifts and Grants	11.5%	2.9%	21.9%
Endowments	4.6%	0.9%	8.9%
Other	9.7%	10.8%	8.3%
	100.0%	100.0%	100.0%

* Council for Financial Aid to Higher Education.

In view of the great difference in the sources of income between public and private higher education, to consider the income of all higher education and project future income on that basis is likely to be misleading. Income from government, as it relates to public and private institutions, is not comparable either. The greater part of the public money going to public institutions is appropriated by the state governments. Tax funds in support of private higher education are almost entirely from the national government.

As matters stand, if the vastly increased enrollments are accommodated for the most part in public universities and colleges, it is to be expected that the funds to provide for their education will come largely from public treasuries. On the other hand, if private colleges expand enrollments greatly, the funds to enable them to do so will be expected to come from increased current gifts, enlarged endowments or student fees. It is an over-simplification to forecast future revenues through extrapolation of the four basic sources of collegiate income. The wishes or preferences of individual economists or educators will not be a determining factor either. In our laissez-faire system of higher education, much will depend upon who takes the initiative. For example, there have been eight new medical schools established in the past 20 years, five public and three private.

TUITION AND STUDENT FEES

Tuition now constitutes slightly more than 46 percent of the income of private institutions, owing to a rise of almost 165 percent since 1950. The trend toward heavier enrollments in public higher education may be a reflection of this tuition increase. Some of the strongest private universities are already concerned lest they have priced themselves out of the market for all students save the very wealthy or the heavily-subsidized, brilliant ones. Fees in public institutions have been upped 129 percent in the last nine years. Recent fee increases in private colleges and sometimes in public ones have been made out of necessity to meet existing financial exigencies. They have not always been made with a full view of the consequent imbalance that might result between public and private higher education. They have not taken into account either the limiting effect higher tuition might have upon the numbers of young people attending college. Signs are apparent that because of higher educational costs, more young men are going to college on a part-time rather than a full-time basis. It is a wasteful public policy that keeps the most capable youth out of college or in college part-time while they earn their way at jobs commanding less than their full talents.

In the last three years there have been strong advocates of the idea that all higher education must secure needed funds by selling its product at true or full cost. Some considerations have caused the full-cost advocates to retreat to a position of advocating simply higher tuition. By charging full cost, the argument went, universities and colleges could pay adequate salaries, maintain and enlarge plants and otherwise operate in a "business-like" way. A built-in incentive is claimed thereby for efficiency. Costs would be kept as low as possible, thus attracting students to a particular institution which contrived to offer the most for the price. Supposedly, education would be marketed à la Madison Avenue. Presumably, a baccalaureate degree at University "X" might be pushed because it "teaches good like a university should."

1. *The Full-Cost Tuition Plan*—There is enough appeal in the high-cost tuition plan to warrant its further discussion.

American higher education through its professional schools has had some experience with self-supporting and proprietary ventures. Years ago the potential earnings of doctors, dentists, and lawyers lured students. Yet, their self-supporting professional schools on the whole were shameful. Recall the sad condition of medical education when it was self-supporting and as it was revealed for its lack of quality by Abraham Flexner in 1910. Higher education in the health sciences achieved respectability on this side of the Atlantic only after student fees were richly supplemented by both public and private grants.

If all higher education were to start *de novo,* the high tuition principle might be a little more feasible, but not at this juncture in our history. With endowments distributed as unevenly as they are, and the happy results they have brought to a few institutions—great faculties, accomplishments, and accumulated prestige—an inequitable situation exists. The full-cost tuition plan would not lead to greater educational strength in a greater number of institutions which is what the country so much needs. The heavily endowed universities and colleges which could afford to charge the most and whose present costs are high, have a built-in subsidy. They would have an opportunity to set tuition as their singular self interests required. On the other hand, colleges that are poorest, often with small endowments and needing increased enrollment to provide a truly sound education at something like an optimum per-student cost of instruction, would have to charge the highest fees. They, for years to come, would have the least to offer in product. Furthermore, students who traditionally go to institutions lacking prestige and resources are commonly hard-pressed financially and need subsidization either directly or indirectly.

2. *Scholarships*—Admittedly, a corollary of high tuition has been the

advocacy of scholarships offered under several different schemes. During 1958-59 the colleges themselves offered $225 million in all kinds of financial assistance to students. From outside sources another $75 million was contributed. However conceived, there are weaknesses in the scholarship plans. First, today scholarships do not mean brilliance so much as they do financial need. The lack of a scholarship seldom means no chance of an education, but it may mean inability to go to a more costly and prestigious institution. However poor the relatively wealthy college may declare itself to be, there is such interest in securing the ablest students that funds are diverted from salaries and operations to provide attractive scholarships for bright but impecunious students. Secondly, there is the highly complicated procedure of evaluating relative need. This necessitates a costly bureaucracy, each bureaucrat with a combination of the skills of a social worker and an internal revenue agent.

To be effective, scholarship application forms must be complex and comprehensive. They must be carefully analyzed and evaluated by skilled personnel to determine the ability of parents to support a son or daughter (sons or daughters) in college. Family size and assets in homes, automobiles, securities and bonds, bank accounts, real estate, insurance and current annual earnings must be viewed in terms of current expenses, indebtedness, taxes and retirement circumstances. Moreover, these family declarations must be validated to the fullest extent possible through inquiry of friends, neighbors, clergy and local school personnel. The time and staff required for such detail is often underestimated. To hand out scholarships without such careful investigation is perhaps to hand out money where it is not needed. Such a practice would reflect adversely upon all colleges and universities for having acted irresponsibly with public funds.

3. *Tax-Forgiveness Plans*—Another scheme for the distribution of scholarship money is to give special rebates to taxpayers who are confronted with unusual costs in the education of their children. This approach is wasteful and governmentally irresponsible. It takes money from the public purse, but not by responsible governmental authorities appropriating on the basis of relative needs of the country. It is hard to conceive, too, how such tax relief could be given under a progressive income tax structure without giving greater advantage to those with high incomes, thus inverting the ability-to-pay theory of taxation. Furthermore, to appropriate monies through tax forgiveness for education, worthy as it is, would be to open a kind of Pandora's Box. Other services might set forth equally appealing claims. Tax revenue would be dissipated. Legislative bodies which are elected by the people must have

adequate resources to finance functions indispensable to modern civilization. To appropriate, in effect, through tax deductions is no way to determine whether the tax dollar brings a reasonable and to-be-expected return in services. Moreover, tax remission helps the parents to educate their children; it does not necessarily provide added collegiate revenue.

4. *Tuition Vis-a-vis Public Higher Education*—Not only the private institutions and their clientele have had a built-in subsidy to tuition. So have publicly supported ones. Psychologically, the population in large areas of our country, such as the Middle West and the Far West are not conditioned to high fees. Citizens in such regions would be as shocked by the idea of paying, directly, the true cost of higher education as they would be to awaken some morning to find that all their roads were toll ones. If existing low-fee public universities and colleges were to increase fees drastically, indications are that already existing pressures to extend free public high schools for at least two more years would be greatly stepped up. Such upward extension of the high school would aggravate the problem of higher education for two reasons: often such operations would be too small to be economical if all costs were taken into account; they could not attract qualified faculty, if quality is given anything like its proper consideration.

One might, also, ask why higher education should be singled out for financing on a "cost to consumer" basis. Hospitals, parks, museums, libraries, symphonies and a host of other activities, perhaps less socially and economically significant, are supported in part by appropriations, by endowments, insurance schemes, or through public giving—Red Feather and otherwise. Each Boy Scout or Campfire Girl should first begin to pay the true cost of membership.

5. *What of Graduate Fees?*—The full-cost tuition plan reveals a particular weakness when related to graduate education. The difference between the charge to students and cost of the education given is greatest at the graduate school level. Fellowships, remission of fees and subsidization of instructional cost by research grants and by universities help bridge the enormous gap. With all this subsidy, graduate students are in short supply. The reason is obvious. The Bachelor of Science in Engineering who enters upon work for the Doctorate gives up, it is estimated, four years of earning and upwards of $20,000. Even the staunchest advocates of the high tuition principle are strangely silent with respect to making graduate students pay their own way.

Recognition has grown that higher education benefits not only the recipient but society as a whole. Educated men and women strengthen the nation as well as themselves. Admittedly, the educated individual earns more in his lifetime; nevertheless, through progressive taxation he ultimately pays not only for the cost of his education but, in considerable part, for governmental services as well. He is also a prime contributor to eleemosynary institutions. In Russia, where in philosophy and to some extent in fact, everything is for the benefit of society rather than the individual, the individual student, because of his expected contribution to society, is not only given a publicly supported collegiate education but a stipend while pursuing it.

6. *Total Cost of Going to College*—Most of those proposing higher fees fail to recognize that tuition and fees are only part of the cost of going to college. In the aggregate, the cost of board, books, room rent and travel, is commonly a little more than double the tuition charge. These higher costs not only reflect inflation but the amortization costs of dormitories that universities, especially public ones, have been compelled to finance through bond issues. According to a United States Office of Education report, the median gross expense to each student in 1957 was $1,219 per year; $1,674 in private institutions and $1,120 in public. Over half of all students attending college in 1957 spent between $800 and $1,700. When one recalls that the average family income in the same year was a little more than $6,000—the cost of higher education for the average family approaches the prohibitive as far as father's pocketbook is concerned. About half of our college population comes from families in the average income bracket—about 80 percent of them from families where the income is under $10,000. Only about 10 percent of American households' income is above that figure. It is estimated that even by 1970 only 23 percent will be so fortunate. Certain as are the heavy expenses of a college education for a high percentage of our middle income group, three out of five families do not have educational savings plans of any kind. Among those who do, the median amount laid up each year for this high purpose is only $150!

Even now students are finding it necessary to borrow more heavily to meet the costs of their education. In the last three years borrowing to meet collegiate expenses has risen three-fold, from $40 to $120 million. With the large number of children in the postwar family, the youngsters are assuredly going to have to borrow more and earn more to help themselves if costs rise only modestly. It also must be recognized that as the percentage of youth in the college-age bracket going on to college rises, most of the students will come from lower income families. The danger inherent in forcing students into large indebtedness to attend college is that they won't go. As a nation the United States can ill afford the waste of man- and woman-power that occurs when children with the best brains are not educated to perform their optimum function.

It is a well-documented fact that between 100,000 and 200,000 high school pupils in the top quarter of their class fail to go to college primarily because they lack the necessary funds.

7. *Some Increases Necessary*—Before one puts up a "Go Slow" sign on financing the future of higher education through high charges to students, one must recognize that the parents who constitute a large segment of the public are somehow going to have to meet this expense. But to ask the parent, plus such self-help as his offspring can supply, to shoulder the cost through direct payments in the concentrated period of ten years when his "planned" family of three or four offspring are in college may be unrealistic. Nevertheless such a reputable economist as Professor Seymour Harris suggests fee increases that would jump tuition from 25 percent, as at present, to 40 percent of collegiate income. Dr. Robert Calkins proposes more moderate increases which would keep this source exactly at the present 25 percent. Even these projected fee increases must be weighed against such roadblocks as a tradition of heavily subsidized private higher education and tax-supported public higher education, larger families, and the limited ability of the average American family to meet such costs as college educations already present. If these roadblocks cannot be overcome, other means of financing will have to be found to meet the national necessity for educated manpower. Nevertheless, some increases in student fees must be weighed in seeking more revenue for higher education.

VOLUNTARY GIVING

For the reasons cited, higher charges to students do not seem to give full promise of the needed funds for higher learning. What are some other possibilities from private sources? There are some which have shown remarkable potential in recent years. Gifts and grants, both corporate and individual, have about tripled in dollars in less than a decade. The percentage of collegiate income from this source has doubled from ten percent in 1949-50 to over 20 percent in 1960. Endowment income has, over the same period, risen dollar-wise about 100 percent. But as a percentage of collegiate income, it has remained about constant at five percent.

1. *A Tradition of Giving*—Harvard College, America's original institution of higher learning, got under way with a gift from John Harvard. It was subsidized, too, from public monies for many years. Eventually gifts, particularly in the form of endowments, given during the burgeoning economy of a rapidly industrializing nation in the 19th century, were so plentiful as to enable some colleges to forgo public subsidy.

Many more private colleges were founded, sustained and sometimes enriched. This philanthropic development was uniquely American. It owed a great deal to the Christian ethic as well as to the virginal resources of a new world, thinly populated, isolated from European wars, and requiring so little of government that only a small percentage of the great entrepreneur's income was taken by way of taxation. Just before the Great Depression of the 1930's, endowments counted for a greater part of higher education's income than any time since—about 15 percent as against the present five percent.

2. *Endowments*—There are several difficulties, obviously, in looking upon income from endowments as being of significance to all higher education in meeting its enlarged responsibilities of the near future. First, there is the matter of endowment distribution. Forty percent of the nation's almost 2,000 colleges and universities have no endowments at all. Of the nearly 1,100 institutions reporting some endowments, 80 percent of the funds was held by 909 private institutions and only 20 percent by the nation's public institutions. Whether private or public institutions are considered, the bulk of the principal and income from endowments is highly concentrated. Out of an estimated total of $3.8 billion in book value of endowments held by 200 major institutions recently surveyed, $2.6 billion or 65 percent belongs to 17 colleges and universities—less than one percent of the total number of institutions and only seven percent of collegiate enrollments.

If endowment income does increase in the next ten years from its present $160 million to $270 million, as the Council for Financial Aid to Education hopes, it will still have declined even in private institutions as a percentage of their income. Moreover, endowment growth and distribution will probably bear little direct relationship to the distribution of enrollments. Such large drives for new capital as Harvard, Princeton and M.I.T. are making, are not particularly based upon a growing student population.

3. *Other Philanthropy*—Voluntary giving from foundations, alumni and friends and corporations amounted to $833 million in 1956-57. This was for all purposes; it included scholarships which, incidentally, do not help the colleges but aid students. These benefactions now constitute about 20 percent of the income of higher education. Without question, this has been higher learning's fastest-growing source of income. It has led to confident predictions that voluntary giving will continue to grow greatly and will constitute as important a source of income in the future as it does today. To do so it will again have to double. The potential of voluntary giving cannot be altogether judged from its splendid recent record. Its meteorlike rise in the past decade

was possible for several reasons. Prior to that time almost nothing had been contributed to higher education by corporations. The largest of the foundations, Ford, had not yet entered the collegiate scene, and a multitude of smaller foundations had not yet gotten under way. Further, until recently, alumni giving was assiduously pursued in a highly organized way in only a few of the more sophisticated private colleges and universities.

4. *Gifts an Unstable Source*—Welcome as they are, gifts are not without weaknesses as a basis upon which to build the future revenues of higher education. First, they are too unstable a source. Faculty cannot be hired and programs instituted on the basis of funds which, owing to economic fluctuations, might not be forthcoming in the same magnitude in a slight recession year. Secondly, as is the case with endowments, the distribution of gifts favors the already strong and relatively well-supported institutions. For example, 60 percent of all foundation grants went to 65 major private universities. Third, many corporations and alumni make no contribution at all. Thus, the burden is not shared equally. Nationally, only 25 percent of alumni give anything at all to their alma mater. A few of the national foundations give nothing at all to higher education. Fourth, voluntary gifts are, to too great an extent, restricted for some pet project of a donor or for a *quid pro quo* relationship between a corporate donor and an institution. It seems that those who give to higher education voluntarily often want to buy tinsel for the Christmas tree of learning. Too few understand that help is most needed to purchase and nourish the all-important tree.

For the many reasons discussed, there are misgivings about charges to students and voluntary philanthropic approaches providing funds in the amounts and patterns required by enrollments. This necessitates consideration by those really seeking a solution of an enlarged role for governments.

STATE AND LOCAL GOVERNMENTS

As the conditions for civilized existence become ever more sophisticated, activities once privately and individually handled are of necessity taken up by governments. The growth of cities caused private wells and privies to give way to municipal water and sewage disposal systems. Before the poverty and distress of the Great Depression became overwhelming, welfare services were provided in large measure by private agencies philanthropically supported. Now governments—local, state and national—have by far the greatest responsibility both for welfare functions and for their support. Higher education bears a direct relationship to national security and economic prosperity. The first has always been a concern of the national government, and the second seemingly is fast becoming so. This relationship plus the impending tidal wave of students suggest that government monies—even from the Treasury in Washington—will be of greater importance in higher education's future.

The big question is whether the tax source is to be state or federal. If state and local governments do not or cannot provide the needed funds, the safety and well-being of the United States will ultimately make it necessary for the federal government to do so. In today's world our higher educational enterprise, whether operated privately by the states or even by municipalities or school districts, is national in its essentiality and international in its consequences.

Our Constitution of 1787 reserved higher educational activities to the states or to the people rather than specifically delegating them to the national government. At that time the central government was given only such powers as were required under late 18th century conditions for an essentially rural country to carry on its affairs. First the Industrial Revolution and now the scientific one have placed strains upon the division of powers between the states and the nation under one federal system. If the Constitution were to be written under today's circumstances, educational authority might be enumerated along with the power to coin money, regulate foreign and interstate commerce and other authority granted to Congress in Article I, Section 8. The government of the United States has been able to meet its greater responsibilities in the 19th and 20th centuries owing largely to the broad interpretation given its few specified powers. It must be remembered—especially by those who would believe that there is something unconstitutional about the federal government aiding higher education directly—that the central government has the power to tax and to spend for purposes not specifically delegated to it, provided that those purposes are for the "general welfare" or the "common defense." Thus federal subsidy to education doubtless is constitutional. Although Congress has supplied money to the land-grant colleges and universities without constitutional challenge for almost 100 years, the state governments will, because of tradition and general preference, probably be looked to initially to provide for the nation's colleges and universities.

1. *Financial Competency of the States*—Whether the 50 commonwealths are likely to meet this challenge is at bottom a question of governmental and financial competency. The layman might think the solution to future enrollments and the adequate financing thereof simply requires the states to tax and appropriate the revenues to higher education. The chances of this happening expeditiously are not good. The variations

in wealth among the 50 states are great. Per capita income, which is about as satisfactory an index as exists of the ability to support the functions of government, varies tremendously from the so-called rich states, such as Delaware, Connecticut and New York, to the poor states, such as Mississippi, South Carolina, West Virginia and Arkansas. The amount of revenue per capita available to the states through taxation in the year ending June, 1959, was on the average $91.70; the poorest state had $55.60; the richest $149.94. Often the poorest states are already making a tax effort out of proportion to ability to pay, and to expect them to do substantially more is unrealistic. Basically, this accounts for much of the extension of federal aid. The concentration of college age population, furthermore, is not always directly related to the wealth of the commonwealths. State taxes in fiscal 1959 ranged from $1.8 billion in California to $38 million in New Hampshire.

There are also many other difficulties growing out of the tax structure.

First, the high level of taxation to meet the national government's expenditures, arising initially from the depression and more recently from hot and cold wars, has engendered stout resistance to higher taxes at all governmental levels, particularly state and local. This is understandable enough. In 1929 all government taxes absorbed only eight percent of the Gross National Product. Today governments take over 28 percent. Thirty years ago the federal government required only one-third of the total taxes levied. Today the federal government requires roughly 75 percent of total tax revenues. Although taxpayer resistance comes to focus most strongly in our 50 state capitals, since 1946 state and local governments have increased tax revenues by 200 percent and their indebtedness by 250 percent. Moreover, the G.N.P., in the same years, rose only about 90 percent, causing the states' tax share to rise from 5.9 percent to 8.7 percent of the G.N.P. In spite of such effort, the states in recent years have had only 13 to 15 percent of the tax dollars. Unless there is general disarmament, no great relief from the federal tax burden is likely. All-in-all, the states face extraordinary difficulties in raising additional taxes, even in increasing their bonded indebtedness.

Second, state tax systems are generally of the regressive variety. Direct rather than indirect levies are commonly employed. These features make the liberal elements, who generally admonish the government to meet service needs, reluctant to have the states levy new taxes if they are not based on ability to pay. Organized labor's position in Michigan is illustrative. With the progressive taxation principle followed so completely by the federal government and with the same taxes so often levied by several levels of government, conservatives try to maintain the status quo. For example, 80 percent of the taxes in the ten major tax categories are collected at two or more levels of government. To add to the difficulty, state tax sources usually do not relate directly enough to the growth of the economy.

Third, the states, out of practical considerations, are limited both in their choice of tax levies and in their rates, owing to competition among themselves. They are all trying to attract and hold industries.

Fourth, state constitutions preclude some commonwealths from fully exploiting certain tax sources. During the depression some constitutions were amended to restrict the use of the property tax. Strict court interpretation of so-called uniformity clauses in tax articles of state constitutions have proscribed the use of graduated income taxation in such states as California, Illinois and Michigan.

Incidentally, state constitutions, too, have quite unrealistic debt limits or have prohibited bonded indebtedness altogether. In certain states, these limits, sometimes written over a century ago, were meant to reduce the folly of extending public credit to canal companies. They now work against properly spreading capital outlays over the several generations who will use them. Another state constitutional limitation related to finances, but different in kind, adversely affects the development of universities. Kentucky, for example, has a salary limitation of $12,000 for all state officials and, peculiarly enough, university personnel were interpreted as coming within the limitation. Conceiving university faculty as in the same category with temporary, part-time, political office-holders, who have business, farm or professional incomes to fall back on, may well leave a state with a university but no professors in this day when intellectual talents plus extensive training are required by industry and the federal government as well as education.

Fifth, special interest groups, dissatisfied with legislative appropriations usually tightly controlled by state finance committees, have secured, sometimes by constitutional amendments, the dedication of certain lucrative taxes to their special interest—highways, fish and game activities or old-age pensions. This unsound fiscal practice has been justified on the basis of relating the tax collected to the corresponding expenditure, i.e., gas taxes for highway construction. Thus, the so-called state general fund has been whittled away. Legislatures, if they would, are not able to budget for state services on the basis of proportionate need.

Finally, federal grants-in-aid on a matching basis also have distorted state expenditure patterns and will continue to do so. If a particular function, such as higher education, is not one of the many presently receiving matching grants, it is in a weak position to compete for its share of any new state revenues developed. For example, higher education in 1920 and in 1930 received a substantially higher percentage of the state tax dollar than during the New Deal or post World War II eras. On the one hand, few of the states have matched to the full extent all the money that might be received under federal formulae. Pressure groups operating in Washington, state capitals and county seats incite each state to take advantage of every nickel available. On the other hand, legislators are pressed by their hometown constituents for further subventions from the state treasuries for local functions. Such subventions have jumped by 250 percent in just over a decade; for secondary and elementary schools by 325 percent. Activities primarily dependent upon the state, such as higher education, have been and stand to be ground between the upper millstone of federal fiscal policy and the nether millstone of state aid to local governments. At best, public colleges and universities are going to have to share available funds or even additional ones with many other governmental functions. All functions claim to have fallen behind and to be confronted with larger responsibilities to more people.

2. *Governmental Competency of the States*—Certain fundamental governmental weaknesses common to most states also will hamper their meeting higher education's needs.

In general, state legislatures have not been regularly reapportioned. Legislatures over-represent rural areas and under-represent urban majorities. It is expecting the incredible of human nature to ask the most rural, conservative and provincial interests in our commonwealths to respond promptly, generously and with complete understanding to the needs of higher learning because the *nation's* economic system and scientifically oriented common defense depend upon it. Responsibilities for these larger considerations have not heretofore been conceived as belonging to state government.

By state constitutional arrangements executive leadership is not concentrated in the governor but is scattered among other elective state officials. A plural executive cannot be held closely accountable by the people. Pressing problems can be ignored with relative impunity and often are. Hence, many federal matching grants have come into existence to compensate for backwardness on the part of state governments. Where governors would exert leadership, they, being elected by a statewide popular vote, are often of one party and the legislatures reflecting rural constituencies are commonly of the opposite.

The states, too, are the heart of the organization of American political parties. Partisan concern is often with small maneuvers to gain advantage in the next national election rather than with consideration of vital public policies calling for farsightedness in the national interest. Of all the states' activities, higher education is generally—and must remain so—least amenable to developing political advantage. Colleges don't distribute jobs on a patronage basis or show partisan interest in politics. Most undergraduates don't vote yet. The colleges have no P.T.A.'s.

One further pertinent consideration. The state's role in financing higher education's future is somewhat prescribed. State monies are usually restricted to so-called public institutions. Under state constitutions it is doubtful whether, even if treasury conditions permitted, they could make appropriations for private institutions. At least half the states are expressly forbidden to aid sectarian schools, or to make appropriations to any college or university controlled by a church. Where there is no specific constitutional restriction, there lurks uncertainly in the background the fourteenth amendment of the Federal Constitution. This amendment has been interpreted by the Supreme Court as applying to the states the limitation laid upon Congress by the first amendment that no law shall be made respecting an establishment of religion or prohibiting the free exercise thereof. A number of non-sectarian, independent institutions do report income from state and local governments. However, the total amount is small, usually less than three percent of the educational and general income of all private institutions. That the percentage is this high is owing to special peculiarities in the structure of higher education in New York, Pennsylvania, Vermont, and Maryland. The remainder represents, primarily, payment for services rendered and goes largely to hospitals.

3. *Limitations on the States*—In spite of these fiscal, governmental and other difficulties, a substantial part of the added funds required by higher education will doubtless come from the fifty state governments. It may be unrealistic to assume that what the states may do can be indicated by what they have already done. In ten years state expenditures for higher education jumped from $1.2 billion to $2.2 billion. For the current biennium (1959-61) state appropriations for higher education are, on the average, about 15 percent higher than for the previous two years. Most economists agree the states are going to have increasing difficulty in raising revenues in the next fifteen years at anything like the rates of the recent past. The most notable exception is the optimism of Charles F. Conlon of the Federation of Tax Administrators. In view of the vast state burdens envisaged, particularly for *all* education—elementary and secondary, as well as higher education—it does not seem likely that the commonwealths can raise all the money required for higher education. As we have already mentioned, there seem to be limits to what students (and parents) will voluntarily pay and still go to college. The phenomenal percentage jumps in voluntary

giving also are not likely to be repeated. Likewise, it seems there are ceilings, already reached in some states for the time being, on appropriations.

Issues to Be Faced

WILL THE FEDERAL GOVERNMENT BE TURNED TO?

Is the federal government likely to be called upon to assume more of a financial responsibility for higher education? State government before now has been faced with responsibilities of an entirely new magnitude. When so confronted, the states have often failed to respond with reasonable promptness. Their inaction threatened to weaken the nation. As a result, the people, frustrated at home, by-passed the state capitals. In Washington they were met by legislative bodies with a broader outlook, more representative of the whole people and with a greater sense of responsibility for the national strength. The President, a single chief executive, with unquestioned responsibility for the national well-being was usually even more responsive than Congress. Federal aid was the goad used to stimulate the states to needed legislative programs and to expenditures commensurate with the situation.

PRESENT FEDERAL PARTICIPATION

Up to now federal aid to education has developed only with respect to somewhat peripheral activities. In the public schools, aid has been given for school lunches, vocational education, and to school districts where federal military and other installations have created unusual enrollment burdens. It is paradoxical that vocational education has been accompanied by considerable federal programming and control. Yet, such involvement from Washington has not caused resentment of federal aid among the very elements (business and industrial leaders and their trade associations) who are the most vocal opponents of federal aid to education in general.

In higher education, except for modest instructional grants to landgrant institutions, federal money has been available for research, overseas programs, specialized training programs for personnel, for example in nursing and vocational rehabilitation and, more recently, for loans, fellowships, subsidies to graduate education, language training programs, aid to science teacher training and a host of other activities. Federal funds for buildings have varied from outright matching grants under

P.W.A. in the Depression to federal purchase of long-term revenue bonds for income-producing facilities and occasional helpful grants for the housing of research. There have been advocates and critics, commendation and criticism of one and all these programs.

Private as well as public higher education has, however, generally taken advantage of these funds. These programs have been somewhat incidental to the teaching function, which is prime in all but a few great universities. Heads of the latter benefiting from the federal programs and moneys have, at the same time, frequently voiced stout philosophical opposition to federal aid to higher education. They are seemingly blandly unmindful of their inconsistent position. Such statements are reiterated by leaders of smaller and less prestigious colleges who are unaware that research funds in such large amounts are being received and have become indispensable to the teaching activities in these sophisticated institutions whose lead they follow. It may just be that leaders of all types of collegiate institutions concerned not to offend large donors and conservative trustees—the latter understandably allergic to the thought of further governmental expenditures—are loath to make either objective study or public pronouncements concerning federal support of higher learning.

Collegiate income from governmental sources, almost entirely federal, being received by independent institutions is about 15 percent of their total income. Since less than two hundred of the nation's colleges have the capacity for research, the remainder are receiving almost no governmental funds although they may have the lowest standards of institutional living. One must conclude that a few private universities and colleges must be receiving a much higher percentage of their total support from federal programs. The general situation is well illustrated by the distribution of the National Science Foundation and the Public Health Service grants. The majority of colleges which, of course, have no organized research receive nothing. Ten universities, seven of them private ones, received about one-third of the total grants of these two agencies.

COMPLEXITY AND DIFFICULTIES OF CURRENT PROGRAM

Commonly, federal programs are conceived and executed without aid to higher education being even a secondary purpose. They are primarily a device for a federal department securing personnel, information or service. Federal dollars in a large measure are but *quid pro quo* for higher education's response to the needs voiced by government. As has been emphasized in Chapter 3, the payments sometimes have not covered the demonstrable costs to the institutions. Because federal money is available only for such specialized purposes, it has affected the very nature of higher education, altered markedly the teaching emphasis, given colleges new directions and responsibilities, and obviously rearranged their financial structures.

It is not likely that any one complex institution has completely analyzed the extent and diversity of its grants from the federal government. As a result, and as we have already seen, they cannot adequately answer such questions as: Are these grants and contracts good for the institution as a whole? Are they developing the university in the directions it would have taken if the officers of the university had had an equivalent amount of undesignated money? Has the added federal money advantageously affected the undergraduate program with respect to teaching and course content? What will be the effect of still more such money upon the institution's development and control?

Seldom, indeed, does one hear complaints of direct interference of the heinous kind so much feared as a counterpart of federal dollars. But, because the money comes from so many diverse federal sources, each one initiated and executed without a relationship to the other, none of them responsible for their total effect upon the nation's colleges and universities, higher education as a whole may be weakened in its ability to do its prime jobs. The end result could be higher education's meeting a lot of disparate and external needs (medical and other research, scientists, military personnel, nurses, and esoteric linguists), but having its own financial needs and other basic requirements for orderly existence unmet, shaved and disrupted. Higher education may become an amorphous giant, unable or uninterested to instruct twice as many students, controlled neither by the central government nor by the trustees and faculties traditionally responsible for it.

One of the greatest difficulties in establishing a comprehensive policy and a proper organizational relationship between the United States government and higher education is the existing and diverse pattern of federal subsidy. Federal funds now in the neighborhood of two billion dollars annually are distributed through many distinct federal agencies, each with a separate program and its own policies and objectives. These are often overlapping or inconsistent. For example, the long-established Reserve Officers' Training Programs are quite discrete for each of the three military services. President Eisenhower's Committee on Education Beyond the High School in its second report issued in July, 1957, recognized the confusion both within the government and for the universities and colleges. It urgently recommended that machinery be constituted to at least make "a continuous and orderly review and development of the national, intergovernmental aspects of education beyond the high school." Over two years have passed since this recommendation was made. Surprising as it may seem, only recently has staff been secured to implement this obvious first step toward a rational over-all program.

Under present conditions the national government does not know exactly what all its policies with respect to higher education are, not to mention classifying and ordering them. This is essential for the proper control of governmental activity by both the Congress and the President. The present discrete administrative arrangements may well mean less control by the elective branches of government than would exist even if the government should divest itself of the usual instruments of control (budgeting, purchasing, accounting and audit) under an arrangement similar to the British University Grants Committee. Moreover, under the existing system, it is not possible for the federal government to know or to ascertain what effects its programs are having upon the total structure of American higher education.

PROBLEMS CREATED FOR HIGHER EDUCATION

This piecemeal approach is unsatisfactory not only from the standpoint of sound government but also from that of the colleges and universities. In dealing with the federal government, higher education has no single focal point at which to present its problems. To realize the possibilities for federal support, a university needs—and a small college cannot afford one—a full-time specialist in Washington, perhaps more than one, who has entries into a dozen or more agencies. The university lacking such a ubiquitous figure is not represented as a university. The relationship becomes one between the professional school deans and more likely between many professors and their professional counterparts in the government establishment. It is not uncommon for federal dollars to be the largest single income item in the financial reports of some of our richest and most important universities. Yet, decisions to accept what appears at first to be a few dollars with modest effects are sometimes not weighed by the policy-making units of the universities.

Requests for grants are often initiated in informal and unofficial arrangements between an agency of the government and some alert professor not responsible for over-all policy of his university but simply seeking a few extra dollars for his work. The small acorn does not seem objectionable at the time that the research is planted on the campus. However, when force-fed by national necessity, it may soon burgeon into an overwhelming oak. Its growth cannot be controlled and it cannot be cut down without harm to the nation and perhaps not without causing disaffection among department members supported by these funds. Often, too, federal programs are begun without any member of a university family being involved. Pressure groups working on Congress to overcome shortages in such fields as nursing or to fight some fatal disease, to give but two examples, secure the necessary appropriations. The universities, more specifically the departments and faculty in them, are asked to carry on a program in these fields. Responsible authority within the universities might, of course, refuse such contracts or grants. Topside there is a realization that some federally initiated programs do not correspond to the priority needs of the university as a whole or even of the departments immediately related to the projects. However, money virtually in hand is hard to refuse in lieu of funds needed but still to be secured. A professor, if disappointed by administration policy, may easily move elsewhere where institutional considerations and priorities do not handicap him.

Federal grant money may do more than change priorities. Because all the costs have not been covered by the supposed federal largess, more essential activities of a university may actually have funds diverted from them. If federal programs do not pay their own true overhead expenses, other university funds must do so. Thus, within the universities activities greatly expanded but inadequately supported by federal subsidy only appear to get richer. Those without subsidy, already poor, in fact get poorer. Those held responsible for each individual university and collectively for all higher education have, under the existing piecemeal federal arrangements, lost control of higher education to a considerable degree.

Yet, there are those who suggest that federal participation in higher education should continue and expand on essentially the pattern of the post World War II period. If the stated weaknesses of the present arrangement do not convincingly argue otherwise, it is only necessary to emphasize that the situation confronting American higher education and the nation today is quite different. The critical problem in the next ten years is not so much one of research but one of teaching larger numbers of students. The present pattern of federal aid is not generally directed toward instruction.

Stumbling Blocks to Direct Federal Support

In spite of a plethora of federal aid for special purposes, a number of historical and governmental conditions have militated against significant federal participation in supporting the basic and fundamental programs of education at any level—elementary, secondary or higher. These can be summed up as follows:

FEAR OF FEDERAL CONTROL

First, there is fear of political control. This fear relates to all government; but it is accentuated when the federal government, because of its nation-wide character, is brought into relationship with education.

Education from the outset has never been considered an ordinary function of government. While historically no other nation has had a greater commitment to universal public education, there has been awareness that education must not be closely regimented and controlled. The fear is that it may degenerate into indoctrination, which is not education at all. From their earliest beginnings, the schools were given their own geographic areas, their own boards of control and a considerable degree of local autonomy. Similarly, public higher education has prospered best when it has been given constitutional independence or inviolate charters. This has permitted public colleges and universities to teach and investigate subjects which might, for the time being, run contrary to popular opinion or custom. It has kept them from partisan and political perversion. In states where independence was legally well established or the tradition of separateness deep, bureaucratic interference has been avoided. Elsewhere, state governments under the guise of efficiency have increasingly invaded the autonomy of public colleges through state controls relative to budgeting, personnel, purchasing, preaudit of accounts, constructions, prior approval of printing, travel —to give the most common examples. According to a Ford Foundation report entitled *The Efficiency of Freedom,* such controls of higher education inevitably lead to interference in areas where freedom is conceded by all as being essential to higher learning with integrity.

If local school authorities or even a state government violate the freedom of schools or colleges, so long as there are thousands of school districts and, more importantly, fifty state governments and hundreds of private colleges, the whole educational system of the nation cannot be subverted or prostituted. The idea is ingrained that to a considerable extent the present strength of American education lies in its decentralization, its diversity and local control, its closeness to the people. There has been awareness, too, that with the granting of funds goes some responsibility for control of expenditures. On the federal level there has been close control indeed since the passage of the Budget and Accounting Act of 1921. For these and other reasons there has been reluctance amounting to insurmountable opposition to the federal government's aiding education, including higher education, in a straightforward, rational manner.

SEPARATION OF CHURCH AND STATE

A second broad reason why the national government had been reluctantly turned to for support for education relates to our heritage of complete religious freedom and its ancillary concept, the separation of church and state. The most common interpretation by the courts of the first and fourteenth amendments to the Constitution is that the federal government and the state governments are prohibited from making grants to religious bodies. This has been assumed to include schools and colleges with a denominational affiliation. Beginning with the Blair Bills introduced into Congress in the 1880's, there have been many abortive attempts to obtain federal support of the general program of education in the public schools. The failure of proposed legislation to pass suggests an impasse. Any bill *without* aid to parochial schools cannot secure a majority in Congress. Any bill *with* aid to parochial schools seems likely to be defeated but by opponents from two other directions—those who would keep Washington's expenditures down plus those determined to keep separate church and state. Owing to mounting enrollments in parochial schools—now from 35 to 42 percent in some of the great cities—the impasse can only become more of a dilemma.

A similar stalemate is even more likely with respect to higher education. Well over 60 percent of our colleges and universities are private and about 70 percent of these, enrolling about 25 percent of all college students, have some church relationship. Inconsistently, at the very time when a prominent politician with strong minority religious affiliation flatly stated, "There can be no question of federal funds being used for the support of parochial or private schools," the Atomic Energy Commission announced grants to seven colleges and universities unique only in their obvious denominational affiliation—three Roman Catholic, three Methodist and one Jewish. If grants for atomic reactors for teaching purposes do not violate the constitution, would direct general grants to aid instruction in a less specific way do so? Rather than speculate about this constitutional question and use doubts about it as an excuse or delaying tactic, the question should be adjudicated. Then policy decisions could be taken on firmer legal grounds whether or not the desperate financial straits of American higher education should be solved by federal action.

THE SEGREGATION ISSUE

Third, in recent years desegregation has added to the aversion of the people in some states, often in those most needing more money, to turn to Washington for aid. For example, seven of the twenty senators and eighteen of the eighty-one representatives from the ten states singled out recently by the Committee for Economic Development as most in need of federal subsidy, voted against the National Defense Education Act of 1958 which aided education in specialized respects. More recently, ten senators from eight of these ten states voted against the McNamara-Hart Bill (S-8) which provides federal funds to accelerate school construction or to improve teacher salaries as decided by each state.

Congress, as well as the Supreme Court, has responsibility for upholding the Constitution. The Supreme Court has made it clear that segregated public facilities are not permissible. It is questionable that the federal government would supply funds to schools or colleges which are not open to all, regardless of race or color.

Problems of Distribution, Organization and Political Philosophy

In addition to tradition and constitution, there are the complicated problems of economic and political philosophy and the machinery for distributing federal funds.

There still resides in the United States a deep-seated antipathy to government. The root of such attitudes lies, of course, in our history. This nation was born in protest against overbearing monarchy. In exploiting the great promise of the Industrial Revolution in a land of virgin resources, restriction of any kind, especially from governments, was unwelcome. Then, too, the economic philosophy of laissez faire emphasized individualism and a limited role for government. Darwin's theories of natural selection and survival of the fittest were later propagated as social and political axioms in the free enterprise economy of a lusty new America. As a part and outgrowth of all this came the idea that the best government was the least government. Such deep-grained attitudes must still be reckoned with whenever a new role for the central government is suggested.

AIDING THE STATES DIRECTLY

A formula for federal aid which could pass Congress and would distribute funds equitably has not been found. There are many reasons for this. The states vary widely in their ability to meet their educational needs. Taxpayers in wealthy states are money ahead if they provide all their own public and higher education out of the state treasury and keep the federal tax dollars in Washington. Some of the more wealthy states are making modest efforts and could do much more to meet their own educational needs. Taxpayers in some states with low per capita income cannot, however, even if they would, provide satisfactory minimum programs, although they are making tremendous taxpayer effort. Congressmen and Senators from states both rich and populous, which could provide for all their own educational needs, are often reluctant to vote federal funds for this purpose in any case. If their own commonwealths are to receive little or no aid, they are even more likely to be against it. They commonly demand a formula distributing federal funds on a straight-out population basis. High-level individuals, like President Eisenhower, and organizations such as the Committee for Economic Development (conservative and yet concerned for education as a not-to-be neglected national necessity) advocate programs of federal assistance only to those states with insufficient resources which are making an acceptable effort. Suggested formulae—out of political realities—usually are a compromise between needs and numbers, and usually penalize states which are not making satisfactory efforts to support education.

In higher education some of the same distribution problems exist to an even greater extent. Such relatively well-to-do states as Massachusetts, New York, New Jersey and Pennsylvania have a very low per capita public expenditure for higher education. The existing pattern of higher education in these states was conceived at a time when a college education was primarily a responsibility of the private sector of our economy. In such commonwealths college-bound students, for the most part, either have gone to privately supported institutions or are exported to public colleges and universities in their sister states. So long as the numbers going to college were relatively small, that arrangement was satisfactory. Ironically, now that it is realized that more young people of college age—even the offspring of the poor—must go to college for the nation's good as well as their own, Senators, such as Case of New Jersey and Clark of Pennsylvania, have been vocal advocates of federal aid. Apparently their confidence is not great that their two wealthy states can or will ever match what other states have already done, not to mention what must be done to meet the tidal wave of new college students.

Any formula would be complicated enough to devise if aid were to go only to public institutions and be distributed among them as each state determined. Admittedly, experience with the land-grant colleges and the federal money they receive for instruction—small as it is—has been a happy one. That type of grant would be a relatively simple way for the federal government to do more in the support of higher education, albeit on a relatively small scale. A greatly stepped up subsidy to public colleges and universities was the recommendation of President Truman's Commission on Higher Education in 1947. Implementing a decision to aid the general programs of *both* public and private higher education, however, would be truly complicated. If the decision were to aid *all* higher education, distribution of federal funds to states on an enrollment basis might not be fair. Private colleges and universities have greater concentration in some regions than in others. The especially prestigious and richer ones enroll students from all parts of the United States. A formula based on the financial resources of the commonwealths would not be satisfactory either. There are rich independent universities in poor states. Some of the commonwealths with rich resources to tax have a predominance of private higher education, with some institutions rich and others churchmouse poor.

AIDING STUDENTS DIRECTLY

That all these difficulties could be by-passed if aid were given directly to the students is a popular notion. Other problems would, however, appear. If federal scholarship aid or even a loan were given to the student directly and only in amounts sufficient to meet current tuition charges, the colleges would not be aided at all but made even more desperate financially. So long as tuitions or fees constitute only a fraction of the true cost of education, the colleges would have more students to educate out of their inadequate existing institutional resources.

The way around this situation might seem to be to aid the students so munificently as to enable tuitions to rise sharply. Fees could more nearly cover full costs. It is not that simple, unfortunately. In both private and public institutions there are existing supplements to fees which vary widely, indeed fantastically. The independent institution has endowments. The second, or public type, has annual appropriations. Both types invite annual gifts. The extent of such subsidization to the education of students has been reflected in the quality and costliness of the programs offered. Costs have, in fact, been determined by the institutional resources on hand. The relatively rich university therefore already has high costs. But it would like, indeed it has an obligation, to pay its faculty of exceptional quality still better. Private institutions could triple rather than double their going fee rate if government scholarships would but subsidize the students. Such institutions might, however, decide not to enroll any more students than they presently do. They would contribute little to the solution of the enrollment crisis, although public funds would be subsidizing them. Moreover, since each college would determine its own cost (salaries, equipment and operating expenses, even building outlays and depreciation), the public treasury could be tapped on an intolerable principle of the more you spend the more you get. Obviously, this arrangement is hard to justify under a system of responsible government.

1. *Special Difficulties for Public Institutions*—Relative to the public sector of higher education, a similar situation might obtain. A few uniquely situated public universities in rich states with a tradition of quality higher education might be in a position to respond quite comparably to independent higher education. Their only fear would be that federal money gotten indirectly through fees would cause their state subsidies to atrophy. Existing federal grants-in-aid to other activities such as health, welfare and highways, assure a continued high level of state participation by their matching requirements. Most public universities and colleges, in all likelihood, would find their legislatures cutting their appropriations and letting the federally subsidized students bear the whole collegiate cost. Owing to their tradition, the public institutions might feel somewhat more obliged to increase their enrollments. They would have no more incentive to keep costs down than would the private institutions.

The only means of assuring a continuance of state appropriation for public institutions and the continued appropriate use of endowment income and gifts for current educational expenses in private institutions would be to take two steps. First, charge *all* students in *all* institutions approximately their full costs. The federal scholarship funds would simply match the state's scholarship to the students in the public institutions and match the private college's subsidy per student from its endowment and gift sources. Second, steps would have to be taken to determine within limits which would win public confidence that each student—and there might be 6,400,000 of them by 1970—was receiving no greater scholarship from either federal and state funds than his financial circumstances warranted. A few well-to-do students might have to pay the full cost of their education out of their fathers' pockets. To make a determination of the financial circumstances of every student would require a great bureaucracy, both on the government's part and the institution's part. The magnitude of the job of evaluating millions of students for financial aid is depreciated sometimes by pointing out that substantial scholarship programs are already being administered by such agencies as the College Scholarship Service and by such populous states as New York, California and Illinois. All scholarship holders in the aggregate total less than one-half million and receive about $300 million. The considerable cost of administering this limited program has not been calculated. But, if it were and extrapolated to apply to twelve times as many students and to distribute billions to them for ultimate payment to roughly 2,000 colleges, a more realistic notion of the immensity of the undertaking might be had.

2. *Dangers to Be Reckoned With*—There are also some dangers to be reckoned with. If all institutional income were directly related to the number of students, two diverse but equally bad practices could develop: first, to get more money colleges might admit students of less than collegiate caliber. Instead of collegiate enrollments approximately doubling, they could rise even higher. Second, those colleges concerned for quality students might, in the heat of competition, not be as conservative and accurate as they should be in ascertaining the exact amount of scholarship required. At least past experience seems to suggest as much.

Some reasonable minimum tuition per student would need to be established. Otherwise, the poor institution with inadequate expenditures per student would not be strengthened by federal funds distributed through scholarships determined by institutional costs. Some colleges in both the public and private category are, at present, spending too little to do an educational job up to a minimum national standard. On the other hand, maximum cost per student to which the federal government would go in matching would, for reasons already given, need to be established.

According to Dr. Richard G. Axt, determining educational costs on some uniform basis, if the G.I. Bill experience is relied upon, is no easy matter. For example, one can imagine the cost-accounting problem created by religious orders which operate a college and have a great part of their teaching done salary-free by devout members. In lieu of compensation they are maintained in varying degrees of material well-being in related convents and monasteries.

AIDING THE INSTITUTIONS DIRECTLY

If federal aid is to go to higher education for its central purposes rather than simply to pay the colleges and universities for services rendered to the national government, the basic question would be whether to distribute the money through payments to over 6,000,000 students or to perhaps 2,000 institutions. Some of the administrative complexities of aiding students directly have already been touched upon. Aiding the institutions directly, especially *all* of them, although feasible, is almost as difficult. They are so diverse in size, purpose, present well-being and aspirations.

As has been done in other American governmental practices and public policies, British experience might be borrowed from. Since 1919 the British Treasury has given annual grants for university education. A body known as the University Grants Committee (U.G.C.) allocates operating and facilities monies to recipient institutions. Admittedly, the British, having an established church, a much smaller country, decidedly fewer institutions, and a highly selective admissions policy, have a much simpler task in subsidizing higher learning. Their approach can but suggest the direction in which the United States government might move if it is to give *significant* financial help to *all* its colleges and universities.

Rather than one highly centralized U.G.C., the United States, with its great number of colleges and a larger percentage of the college-age population actually going to college, might be well advised to regionalize such an undertaking—perhaps establishing a Committee for each region. The latter might correspond to the already established accrediting jurisdictions. The disbursement of funds on a regional basis is more rational than on a single state basis.

Considering nationwide industry, modern transportation and communication, the nation itself, however, probably is the most reasonable unit for planning complex and diverse educational institutions and sophisticated programs. There is good reason to ask today whether the citizens of any one state should as state taxpayers bear the cost of training the variety of specialists that are necessarily to be educated in one complex known as a university. The university graduate under our system of free selection of field of study and subsequent free choice of employment may study theoretical physics in Seattle, Washington, and work in a radiation physics laboratory in Wilmington, Delaware. The practitioner of the old-time learned professions such as law, medicine and theology is more apt to locate in the general section of the country where he received his education. The chemist, the physicist, the engineer, the mathematician, the public health expert, and even the agriculturalist are less provincial. Whether the educated professional man or woman is of the old or new variety, ever fewer are geographically bound to the commonwealth or even the region in which they were educated, especially the outstanding ones. In public health there are only a few universities which have training programs. Their graduates supply the entire United States and most of them work for public jurisdictions. This situation seemed to argue that federal money was justified as aid to schools heretofore financed entirely by state or private sources. A modest federal program was instituted in 1959. It was justified as simply compensation to public health schools for losses incurred in handling government trainees. It might well have been justified upon a somewhat broader basis. The same argument might be made in any number of specialized fields. But the shortcomings of grants on a school-by-school basis by program and their disintegrating effects upon institutions and higher education generally have already been touched upon with respect to other federal grants.

ORGANIZATIONAL AND ADMINISTRATIVE PROBLEMS

The crux of our adopting something like the British U.G.C. system is relevant not only to policy. It is very much related to organization and administration of the grants. The appealing aspect of the U.G.C. approach is the way it is deliberately structured to aid the institutions directly and yet insure higher education's continued freedom. While administrative efficiency and governmental responsibility are necessary, regard for educational freedom is more essential.

To even mention efficiency in the granting of funds to higher education is to hoist a red flag. It has already been pointed out how, under the guise of efficiency, the freedom of higher education is being jeopardized at the state level. Even here the British experience provides a lesson. The U.G.C. consists of well-informed, independent, and distinguished individuals formerly and currently affiliated either directly or indirectly with university education. While they are appointed by the government in office, specifically the Treasury, they enjoy a large measure of autonomy. Apart from the cabinet decision on the total amount the Treasury will give for the five-year period of the appropriation, the government keeps hands off. The five-year appropriation permits continuity and planning and disassociates the universities from the disruptive annual budget process. Roughing out the appropriation need and the expenditure of the funds once appropriated are in the province of the Committee and the universities themselves. Congressmen should note that the U.G.C.'s actions with respect to the distribution of funds among the universities and the institutions' expenditures are not subject to the question hour in Parliament. The British Auditor General does not even audit the transactions. Further, the grants are not made altogether as subsidy to existing programs on some uniform basis. Consideration is taken of the national need to mount greater educational effort in certain localities and in certain areas of knowledge.

What a contrast this fiscal independence of the U.G.C. system provides with the circumstances of our U. S. Office of Education or our National Science Foundation. They have numerous budget hearings at the departmental, Bureau of the Budget and perhaps at the White House levels and again before sub-committees of the appropriations committees in each house of Congress before money is made available by appropriation. Once the money is appropriated, its expenditure is almost intolerably hedged about. Expenditure must be in accord with details written into appropriation laws. These specifications are usually not to satisfy the Congress as a whole so much as some individual Congressman on the committee who has a special pique or a special interest. Pressure groups and self-styled patriotic elements attach amendments and riders such as the oath and affidavit required under Title IV of the National Defense Education Act which makes loans to students. Appropriation committee reports laden with not-to-be ignored instructions and admonitions, departmental controllers and finally the Comptroller General and his General Accounting Office must also be satisfied in the disbursing process. Freedom—not to mention internal administrative efficiency and flexibility within the universities—so necessary to teaching and research might well be smothered under our pattern.

Fiscal responsibility aside, brief experience in the United States under the National Defense Education Act, the National Science Foundation, and the National Institutes of Health, with the use of advisory committees drawn from the universities and similar establishments, albeit on a project basis, suggest that filtering funds to higher educational institutions, numerous as they are, can be done. Doubtless some of the nation's best minds are making the vital decisions as to which research project should be subsidized to lick the cancer menace and which graduate programs in physical biology or some other esoteric field should be enlarged and strengthened in staff, equipment or in fellowships. Such advice is sought and given, however, in a very prescribed context.

No group of like caliber is called upon to consider the objectives of higher education in relation to the nation's well-being. This is no job to be undertaken by harried institutional heads assembled in mass conferences at intervals of once a year by one or another of the several educational associations. Likewise the executive committees or programs and policy committees, meeting for two days or so twice a year do not provide the machinery to do the thinking and planning the situation requires. The people within the government agencies are at once suspect for the assignment and they are too busy with operating responsibilities for the assignment anyway. The best minds in the nation—knowledgeable about higher learning and its organizational requirements, yet not approaching the problems as members of one type of institution or an-other—could well spend their full time upon the assignment. Here we have the germ of an idea not unrelated to Americanizing the U.G.C.

THE PROBLEM OF PERSONNEL

Another difficult problem inherent in federal participation in direct aid to higher education must first be considered. It relates to personnel whatever the organization. The personnel problem is particularly acute, however, if the federal aid is to be administered through an ordinary government department. The caliber of persons needed to give con-fidence to the administration of a full-blown, multi-billion dollar pro-gram of direct federal aid cannot often be attracted in sufficient numbers at the salaries now paid civil servants, even at the super grades. Nor can highly capable people of modest circumstances (as educators so often are) be interested in such posts if they are prestigious but insecure ones subject to political perils. The question which must be faced is whether men can be attracted from the headships or various deanships in our more important colleges and universities to such top national posts. Borrowing personnel on a temporary basis from the universities them-selves is but an expedient. Frequent turnover puts ultimate authority in the hands of the agency's subordinates who are permanent. After a specific program becomes "old hat," the Washington agency concerned must put responsibility upon those available rather than the best qualified. To add to the difficulty, there is little tradition of a specialized, professional educational career service to help recruitment and hold men of high abilities in service such as exists in foreign affairs, public health, or the military. Courageous men and women of the greatest experience, astuteness and wisdom, commanding the confidence of the public, the colleges and their faculties are needed. The very capable people recruited into federal activity during the Great Depression have meanwhile moved on to greater opportunities or have grown near re-tirement. They often have not been satisfactorily replaced in the post-war period. Here may be an administrative activity of the federal govern-ment suddenly rising to an unprecedented level of importance, financially and otherwise, at a time when talent is at the greatest premium and better paid elsewhere.

A Possible Organization for a Democracy

If federal aid is to come, the National Science Foundation in its very name suggests a possible organizational approach for aiding all higher education. If the federal agency related to higher education were developed along the lines of the "foundation concept," such an approach might solve the personnel problem and insure educational freedom as well. A spirit of inventiveness in governmental organization as well as in weaponeering may be required to survive in the space age. The government-corporation device was once adopted to give business enterprises under government aegis the flexibility and freedom to operate with the advantages of private enterprises. More recently, to secure research and development work, the government has contracted for such services. It has been realized that the scientific talent needed could not be secured for the organization devised to do the job directly within the governmental establishment.

Assuredly as much, indeed more, along similar lines might be done for the colleges and universities. Conceivably an "Educational Foundation" in fact, and not simply in name as is the N.S.F., could be created by the Congress. Its endowment would be in the form of periodic lump sum appropriations by the Congress. This Foundation would be given a status of independence similar to the University Grants Committee in Great Britain. The trustees of such an "Educational Foundation" would be drawn very largely from the nation's educational, cultural and scientific leadership on the basis of long-term and full-time appointments. Ideally the board would include presidents and trustees and other administrators, not only of universities but of foundations and scientific and cultural institutions, and distinguished professors. Former institutional affiliation would, of course, be discontinued. Supporting these directors would be a professional staff of highest caliber.

Before such an arrangement is declared to be too grandiose and costly there are some things to be kept in mind. First and foremost is the indispensability of the United States having the best possible system of higher education in the world. Its leadership depends upon it. Second, the size of an organization which would be required to evaluate the financial needs of better than six million students should be envisaged and priced. The autonomy of such a foundation may be thought alarming. The Foundation's actions and hence its responsibility and accountability would be far greater than would be the case if two thousand units of higher education, each determining its own costs and passing them on to the government *via* scholarships were the arrangement. Several of the programs of the federal government that relate to higher education, such as the Division of Higher Education of the U. S. Office of Education and the National Science Foundation might well be folded into the new foundation. Some duplication would thereby be eliminated. The ultimate control of the President and the Congress, the representatives of the people, would be present through the periodic appropriation of lump sums to the Educational Foundation.

* * *

Many issues have been discussed. This is as it should be in a democracy. Only through consideration and reconsideration are problems likely to be resolved. And our problem of financing higher education still remains. It is this: *How can this country step up higher education's share of the G.N.P by 80 percent in the next decade?* That this must be done should not be a conclusion assumed by professors and college presidents. Our whole people must, if effective action is to take place, understand and agree upon the essentiality of education. The considerable support that has already been given to higher education suggests that this approach is not only proper in a democracy but effective. But the next ten years require an ever higher level of understanding and acceptance. The latter must not be in the mind alone. It must be reflected in new dimensions of financing. If the objectives are to be realized, enlarged contributions and taxes from many sources, students, graduates, business, private benefactors and state and federal governments will be required. Controversy over just how, just who, and just when the support will come should not jeopardize higher education when just why is so urgent. The considered judgment of the President of the United States as stated in a speech of April, 1957, is: "The strength of our arms is always related to the strength of our minds . . . Our schools are more important than our Nike batteries, more necessary than our radar warning nets, and more powerful even than the energy of the atom."

5.

National goals and federal means

• Douglas M. Knight

We have looked from several points of view at the nature of the federal government's participation in higher education. We have identified the heavy investment already being made; we have learned something of the history of its many programs, something of their present state, something of the issue that faces us in the next few years. In an admittedly partial and incomplete way, we have identified a few of the complexities, not only of our educational situation but of the many kinds of federally supported programs that help it, or impinge on it, or make use of it— or once in a while, perhaps, merely impede it. We have seen, above all, that these programs use the facilities or the talents of higher education, but are not for the most part designed to support or further it.

176

The Present Problem

By themselves, these various kinds of analysis define our job in this book, but they do not complete it. We must begin to be clear about the national needs we have to meet, the dilemmas and difficulties we face in meeting them, the attitudes we must avoid and the ends we should serve.

It will be the basic assumption of this final chapter that no one view of the problem of federal aid will be adequate to our future, and that no simple plan or "solution" will offer us what we need. On the other hand it is clear enough, from what has been said in Chapters 2, 3 and 4, that the option of whether or not to have federal aid to higher education no longer exists. Even in its present confused form that aid is a major element of the structure of American college and university life. It cannot be argued away; it cannot be removed without intolerable damage to the life of most larger institutions.

This fact, however, does not allow us the comfort of assuming that whatever is, is right. Federal aid has become an organic part of higher education in the country. As a result any change, any development in its pattern will affect the whole tone and temper of everything else that we do, not only to finance higher education but to make it operate properly. As we can see from the intricacies of relationship described in Chapter 3, federal programs in higher education are not the mere ivy on the wall; often they are the stone and the mortar. But as a result we must ask about the organism—first the question of what the relation between education and government should be, and then how we can guide the precise patterns of federal aid so as to assure a minimum of difficulty and a maximum of gain. And we must realize as we answer them that we do not do so from any vantage point of clarity about our purposes in higher education, or our need of government support at some particular point. We must as a country develop enough flexibility of attitude so that we can accept rapid change in educational demand, and drastic increase in the need for support from all sources, without allowing either demand to stampede us into foolishly simplified answers to our complex questions.

The Need for Order

Perhaps a good many of our difficulties at the moment stem from the fact that we have not really found out what we need in higher education, or how we are to finance it after the need has been established. We have,

177

as a result, a good many problems to resolve before we can picture a fully satisfactory fiscal and administrative structure for federal programs. The suggestion of some type of grants commission, which was developed at the conclusion of Chapter 4, has a good deal to recommend it. Before we can look clearly at this or any other structural solution, however, we must inform ourselves about the difficulties of operation which we currently face.

First of all (and obviously enough) there is within the government little coordination of the programs involving higher education. As a result, there is no way to guarantee the efficiency or even the rationality of the whole complex. Each program is the result of some specific need or, as in the case of the National Defense Education Act, a whole bundle of them. Each speaks to a specific occasion rather than a general principle—the lack of graduate students in exotic languages, the pressure for additional undergraduate loan funds, the need for more adequate counseling of high school seniors. There is no way at the moment of getting the "specific occasions" together, of making sure that they accomplish our chief purposes.

Second, there is a good deal of disorder in the triple relationship of Congress, the government bureaus, and higher education itself. To say so is not to criticize the dedicated and highly intelligent work being done both by the national educational organizations and the Department of Health, Education, and Welfare. The Department has no authority over the range of government programs, however, and the national organizations of colleges and universities have no authority even to coordinate and bring to one conclusion the widely divergent opinions of their constituent members. Congress, as a result, can get expert factual information, but finds it a good deal harder to get expert judgment which will lead in any one consistent and coherent direction.

The unhappy consequences of this three-sided difficulty are painfully clear, at times. The hazards of duplication, of competition among bureaus and departments, of sudden, extreme, or even irrelevant demands upon university facilities—all of these unnecessary problems result from the fact that we have no reasonable and effective way of making our plans and decisions with an equal care for the needs and responsibilities of everyone involved.

OATH AND AFFIDAVIT: AN EXAMPLE OF DISORDER

The hazards of government-university interaction are even graver than this at times, however—so grave that they lead to clashes of princi-

ple which create an almost separate area of conflict. Our most spectacular recent example, of course, has involved the loyalty oath and disclaimer affidavit required under certain provisions of the National Defense Education Act. We have been so busy in the debate over the
philosophical and political implications of these requirements that we
have ignored the rather serious problems of assumption and operation
which lie behind the fact that a conflict has had to take place at all.
It might be useful to consider in some slight detail what we have done
during the last few months and what we have failed to do, if only
as a case-study for the procedures we may want to adopt during the next
few years.

Those of us in higher education have tended to assume that the issue
was completely clear cut, and that as a result it imposed no other duty
upon us but that of affirming our virtue, taking a stand, and then moving
back while the dust settled. In some ways this position was right as
well as reasonable; in some other ways it was surprisingly naive—and
most naive, oddly enough, right at the point of our educational responsibility. It looks in retrospect as though we were so concerned to establish
a position that we failed to ask ourselves the teacher's first questions—
whom are we obligated to "inform," and what kinds of information are
relevant to the various groups which need to be educated? We failed
to realize, at least during the first year of our discussion, that in identifying our own attitudes and convictions we had taken only the first small
step toward solving our problem.*

There were three chief difficulties, I think—three failures of education
as I have just defined it. In the first place, we failed to educate ourselves as a potentially coherent, coordinated group of colleges and universities. In the winter of 1959 we expressed ourselves individually to
the Association of American Colleges and the American Council on
Education, but we did not undertake the kind of coordinated national
effort that would have given us a coherent position to develop and then
to maintain. As a result, we moved singly, erratically, and not always
with the clearest motivation. Strong as our logical position of opposition
to the disclaimer affidavit was, we did less than we should have to make
it stronger by wise national cooperation among ourselves. One reasoned
statement of principle, agreed to by fifty colleges and universities, would

---

* If I am to speak so critically about certain of our recent procedures, I
should make clear my own attitude toward this problem. I have been vigorously
opposed to the disclaimer affidavit; and I have felt that the loyalty oath, while
foolish, was also relatively innocuous. It seems to me that the former, once its
implications have been understood, is legally indefensible and morally wrong.
My quarrel, as a result, is totally with the public treatment we have given to
so serious a question, not at all with the question itself.

have accomplished far more than the fifty separate statements of the past year.

In part, of course, we were cautious at first because we did not want to antagonize Congress in its initial steps toward the development of some new and general programs for the support of higher education. On the other hand, this very question of a right relationship to Congress provoked our second chief difficulty; our caution was not followed by any careful and sustained effort to educate Congress in the grave difficulties of a disclaimer affidavit. I question as a result whether the tone of righteous indignation in which we approached Congress did much more than lead some of our friends there to ask why we should put them so strongly on the defensive. If we really wanted to accomplish our end of removing the disclaimer, we stood a very good chance of accomplishing it a year ago through a quiet, moderate and yet united approach to Congress in which we would have asked for no more than was really important. In failing to do this, we failed to recognize the Congressional situation which actually existed.

We failed equally to recognize the difficulties which our position raised for the press and the public. Here, as with Congress, the final responsibility for our difficulties was by no means all ours; but at least we were responsible for understanding the difficulties and working effectively to remove them. In fact there was for months no public understanding of the critical difference between a positive oath of loyalty and a disclaimer affidavit; and as a result the newspaper publicity even in October and November of 1959 hopelessly garbled the two, and confused the general public very badly about the purposes of the colleges. A number of excellent recent articles have helped to remedy this ignorance, but the damage need not have been done at all, if the distinction had been maintained at the start between a harmless loyalty oath and a negative disclaimer which might make a perjurer out of the most innocent undergraduate. Beyond the metaphysics of the matter, it seems clear that we have no right to ask anyone to play the prophet about the organizations he belongs to; he cannot know what they will become, and the disclaimer affidavit implies that he should. It could put anyone of us in an impossible position.

If we failed educationally in these three ways, there is no doubt that Congress failed in showing so little sensitivity to the basic attitudes of the country's colleges and universities, and so little respect for their integrity. It is almost too easy to imagine how a situation might have been corrected, of course; but it does seem clear in this case that a good deal of grief would have been avoided by a little informal discussion between those who drafted the bill in Congress and those who were to administer its provisions in the universities. This is only one of the lessons we should have learned, however. The others, those which directly involve our college and university practice, are far more crucial; and I have discussed our actions of the last fifteen months in such detail only because the future will bring us far more difficult problems to resolve, and we need to profit by our mistakes, rather than allowing ourselves to be surprised when certain things happen—or fail to happen.

We must, in short, resolve the complex problems of decision and operation involved if we are to bring a host of colleges and a swarm of government bureaus into working relationship with one another. Whatever the future interdependence of the two, we cannot afford confusion, discord, or even plain lack of understanding between them. (One of the chief lessons that we have to learn from the University Grants Commission, indeed, is precisely this lesson of honest and constant communication. Whether we can borrow the detailed techniques of the Commission or not, we should certainly take seriously the fact that one of its main purposes is the advancement of reasonable and harmonious university-government relationships.)

It is certainly possible, for instance, to picture in this country a group of able people from Congress, the government bureaus, the national educational organizations, and the universities, who could take some responsibility for coordinating and interpreting our educational plans and policies. As our dependence on the sciences has become more obvious, we have found ways of discussing and supporting their national needs. It is high time, in the interest of order but without the loss of freedom, to consider doing the same thing for all of higher education.

The Task of Cooperation

Perhaps we can consider such a possibility most usefully in the light of our critical responsibilities as I described them in Chapter 1. It is quite clear that most of the present federal programs, though they impinge on our larger educational purposes, were not devised with such purposes in view. That fact makes it seem even more important to have some group which could keep these larger purposes clearly and constantly in focus, not only in the speculative discussion of general educational policy but equally in the questions of national program and operation.

What would such a group find confronting it that might justify its existence? Two major types of questions, I think, in both of which the federal government has a share—and a share which may well grow in the next few years. First, there are the problems of recognition—the identification of major ways in which higher education should meet the responsibilities of the country, both nationally and internationally. Second, there are the problems of support—where and how help needs to be provided if our chief educational purposes are to be met.

It would be a mistake at this point in the country's development to plan anything less comprehensive; for our national goals call for a knowledge of *why* and *where* in education as well as *how* and *how much*. And it would also be a mistake to separate the identification of problems and their support. This has actually been one of our major difficulties until now; too often those with the clearest idea of educational needs have little access to the funds for bringing a wise policy to life, and those with financial control—whether federal, state, corporate, or individual in nature—have had far too little directly to do with the identifying and support of educational goals and purposes. At least it seems impossible on any other basis to account for one of the most disturbing facts of our society at the moment—the small amount of the national income that finds its way into the support of higher education.

We need, then, to resolve a national problem both of the level of support and of the means by which the various kinds and areas of support are to be related. (And we need by implication to recognize that these kinds of support have to be related, not only to our national goals but to one another.) It is important for us to understand how much more than a financial problem we face. It is equally a human one; a glaring example of the fact is that since we have no real order in the financing of higher education, a more and more intolerable burden is falling on the presidents of American colleges and universities. The present state of things with them is worth comment as an example— only one example—of the way we are wasting our human resources because we have taken no trouble to put our financial affairs in order.

It would be romantic, of course, to pretend that the college or university president should be an "educational leader" in the void. Educational policy is financial policy, and the president cannot and should not escape it. It is ridiculous, however, that the wealthiest country in the world should pay lip service to the importance of education and at the same time force its college and university presidents to snatch frantically each year for the money to keep their budgets reasonably in balance. It is not in the least utopian to say that our whole national attitude should be what it is now only in a few blessed spots. "What is the need, and how can we help?" should be the words, not only of a few generous individuals, industrialists, alumni, legislators. They should represent the most irrevocable responsibility we all share.

Until we rectify this situation, we are really saying to ourselves, and to the rest of the world as well, that education is less important for us than a host of other activities in our society—even though those very activities depend upon a high level of vigorous education for their continued existence. College and university presidents should be free to deal with the major issues of education, they should be free to bring new ideas to life; and they should definitely not have to work themselves beyond exhaustion simply to hold their institutions to their present levels of financial effectiveness. The responsibility for seeking out money should not have to be the constant or sole purpose of the president, while the wise deployment of it is certainly one of his major obligations. He should simply be free to do his job.

The time is clearly past when the president, the board of trustees or the faculty can meet these or any other obligations of the institution solely on an individual or isolated basis. Without destroying our personal sense of obligation to one specific college or university, we must reinforce it by national patterns and procedures which can lend support where it is needed most. And in describing these national patterns, and establishing the groups which might bring them into being, we must take account, as I have suggested, both of what we want to accomplish and of what sources of support will make the accomplishment possible.

This will seem like an almost automatic or inevitable suggestion, perhaps; but in fact we do not have such groups at the moment. None of our organizations exists to solve basic types of educational problems; instead they are usually formed to lend particular support to certain kinds of solutions, or to certain groups with particular interests. The great organizations which lend private support to the sciences, for example, have no orderly way of communicating about total national needs with the National Science Foundation and the Institutes of Public Health. Our work in support of international education is done by a hundred organizations in a hundred different ways. There is no doubt that we need such multiple support, but it seems that we also need some way of establishing and judging its total significance.

The pursuit of significant purpose, in short, which is so important a part of our national self-analysis at the moment, has this specific consequence for higher education; we must learn to see ourselves, not in two dimensions but in three. We must first recognize and protect the individual institutions; we must then recognize the many sources of their support; and we must, as a new and third dimension of higher education, recognize our need for organized national direction—a need in which each institution and each source of support can have its part to play. We must meet our complex need, not merely by superimposing new organizations on our present ones, but by raising them to the level and temper of effectiveness which a new situation demands.

Five Kinds of Planning

What will such a new level of organization for higher education have to work on? What will its main obligations be? We have already suggested them in general; they are implicit in the very type of organization we need: first, an obligation to find national direction; and second, an obligation to define national support—its sources and its uses. But we need now to establish in specific terms the areas in which such national groups would work, the kinds of problems they would be concerned with, and the help they could give.

Five of these areas come to mind. In several of them there is work being done, but not on a basis which would make it available nationally, either for the institutions involved or for the large purposes which the government is trying to serve. We might consider them as they move from the most specific to the most general.

The first way in which coordinated national groups or panels could function is in the great discipline areas. We already have this kind of structure in the National Science Foundation; but it is naturally directed toward the country's total scientific need—in which individuals, colleges, and universities have a chance to play their part. We must have in addition a means of integral rather than incidental relationship between the institutions and all sources of scientific support. We need a means of seeing and supporting the sciences in college and university life for what they can be in themselves, as well as for what they can do in support of other enterprises.

To say this is not to be critical of the National Science Foundation or the Institutes of Public Health; they have had to cope with a national obligation and a rate of growth which would give nightmares to Solomon. They have had a profound impact on college and university use of faculty and facilities, while it has not been part of their obligation to deal with the significance, *in context,* of those things they have helped to support or, in many cases, have brought into existence. And we could say the same, of course, for every other source of research funds. It has always been up to the institution to make order from the grants which were secured either by individual faculty members or by research teams. Now under the pressure not only of so many urgent national demands but equally of our long-range national goals, we should find some way of mediating among the many sources of support. We might then be able to control a good deal of the uncertainty which plagues our planning at the moment.

When we talk about the sciences, we can at least speak of coordination among many kinds of support. When we think of the social sciences and humanities, however, we can see that we still have little to coordinate; the level of support for them is pitifully inadequate, and there is still no general public understanding that they are as essential to our welfare as the physical sciences. Any national committee would have first to explain why the help was needed, and then decide where it should come from.

A second national group might take some genuine responsibility for planning the scale and scope of the physical facilities which higher education will need in the next ten years. We should be able, for instance, to say authoritatively, in the matter of college housing, what the American Council on Education and other groups have tried to say recently—that our needs are of a specific magnitude, and must be met. Equally we should be able to say in other areas of physical need—laboratories, classrooms, libraries—that we have plans to make, and that we must move from the making of those plans to our decisions, not about *whether* things can be done, but how, and when, and by whom. It is the very center of existence of the groups I am describing to insist on the national priority of the needs of education.

These needs may be expressed in *a third major way—in the general planning of the purposes which higher education can serve.* Many of us try individually to do something about this sort of planning; but we are too often the fragments of a mosaic which is never assembled. Many committees, for example, do a thoughtful job of planning in restricted areas or for specific purposes. (The educational panel of the President's Scientific Advisory Committee, the Commission on Liberal Education of the Association of American Colleges, the Educational Facilities Laboratory are three widely variant examples of groups which can work effectively for some specific purpose.) No one at the moment has either the time, the facilities or the freedom of access, however, to deal in depth with the whole spectrum of needs to which all of us in education should relate ourselves. Even the greatest universities will need this kind of help in the next ten years, if they are to keep their purposes clear and their resources adequate.

One aspect of our planning is so critical and so complex that it will call for separate treatment by a fourth group. *We must constantly interpret to the public the ways in which education and the rest of our society interact.* Education is more than a means to some other end, after all, more than a mere collection of techniques; it is an attitude, and at its best (as I suggested in Chapter 1) a major aspect of our way of life. It is imperative that we not leave this aspect of our society to chance; there is little left to accident, after all, in the interpretations which labor, management or the churches (to choose only three examples from a thousand) make of themselves for national consumption. And without viewing these self-interpretations cynically at all, it is obvious that they cannot come into being without a great deal of co-ordinated, careful planning. At least as much planning and thought could reasonably go into something of such prime national importance as education; and it should not be in the form of an occasional White House Conference (without even enough allocated funds to complete its study, let alone bring any idea to life). Instead this national need could find expression in a continuing, highly talented commission with the responsibility of asking both central and imaginative questions about the relationships between higher education and the rest of our society. Such a group would have the responsibility of asking where and how the colleges and universities of the country could work with the other chief elements in its social structure. Educational purpose could constantly be seen and interpreted in the setting of national purpose.

But national purpose in the foreseeable future is in its turn only to be understood in a setting of international purpose. Higher education has a clear, present and constant relation to this international context; but if we are to use our resources well and meet our responsibilities adequately, we must have the means, not only of stimulation and mutual support but of *prompt cooperation with like-minded universities around the world. A fifth group or commission should have this as its task.* If the universities of Britain assume a responsibility for some major work in Africa, for instance, they need to have access to those of us here who are deeply but perhaps only fragmentarily involved in the same thing.

Perhaps the need in our international responsibility is for a certain critical mass and weight. The fragments by themselves will not do the job; but taken together, related, pointed toward the struggle for stable freedom in Africa and Asia, they can accomplish something of real value. The issue before us in every area of higher education is exactly the same: we must have somehow the means not only of seeing our problems and our needs, but also of seeing how they can be adequately met. And yet this statement by itself does not cover the final purpose of the five groups I have just described. Problems, needs and resources must always be seen by these groups in their proper setting; the country's heart of purpose must be the end which they both define and serve. The quest for principle and policy, seen as a national obligation but with its particular focus in higher education: this and nothing less must be the job of our central coordinating groups.

The demand is a serious one; we ask these groups to create, in part, the very standards they must use for their own effective planning, judgment, and action. But this, after all, is a need of our whole society at the moment; purpose is no clearer in the shadow-area between politics and the national spirit than it is between education and the country. Nor is it any more crucial. For our understanding as well as our safety we must move toward honest self-knowledge in each aspect of our national life. Our support, our educational planning will be functions of that self-knowledge.

Dangers and Dilemmas

If we are to succeed in so difficult a venture, we must be aware beforehand of the inevitable problems, particularly those which grow from the interaction of government, the foundations, industry, the states, and the individual colleges or universities. These problems, though they are many, will have one central theme; they all depend on our need to protect the creative "best" of the academic life, our need to meet the dual obligation of individual freedom and national purpose. As our need grows for a coordinated setting of support for higher education, so does the danger that those who do the coordinating and who provide the support will unwillingly stifle the very things they intend to promote.

I am speaking here of nothing so clear and evident as academic freedom, narrowly defined. Despite our concern over the current loyalty oath and affidavit controversy, I do not believe that the participation of the government in higher education menaces us with any serious overt restriction on individual freedom. The kinds of restriction I am thinking of are more likely to interfere with our finding new goals, reaching new levels of expectancy, than they are to interfere with our present standards and expectations.

We can best understand such dangers by recognizing precisely what we want to protect, encourage, and stimulate. The most apparent physical aspect of higher education which we must protect is that of multiple financial support. It will be tempting in the next few years to assume that our massive needs can be met *only* by massive federal aid; and that as a result we might as well set aside other forms of financial help in order to simplify matters. Cooperative groups of the kind I have described would be unnecessary, in this way of thinking, and some kind of formula might take care of the distribution of funds.

The most serious danger in such an idea, I think, is in the damage which it would do to the relationship between education and the total economy. Such a relation is crucial, and for two reasons. First, a complex relation to the economy makes somewhat surer the possibility that higher education will get the share of national income which it needs and deserves. Second, and more important from society's point of view, a broad base of support guarantees a national sense of participation in higher education. This participation will not be limited to financial help; but since it includes a solid understanding of the purposes and rewards of higher education, it is likely to keep support at a more adequate level than any simple system could do.

Under a system of educational support which is heavily nationalized, it seems altogether too easy to forget that the level of salaries and facilities in education must keep some parity with those in business and industry. It is possible to set up a scale which relates salaries in education to those in government; but this common European practice does nothing to protect either vocation against the competition of industry and the professions in a period of rapid change. (To put the matter another way, there must be some means of helping salaries in education to respond positively and rapidly to changes in the economy. Without a broad base of support, it seems almost impossible to achieve this end.) Financial support from many sources allows us, furthermore, to bring together major points of view, which can be unified in the support of higher education. It is a major strength of our present system of financing that so many individuals and so many groups have a real concern for the success of colleges and universities. Whatever the added burdens we face, we cannot afford to lose that many-sided interest.

Other dangers develop, of course, from a narrow base of support. Chief among them is the possibility of making decisions of policy that are less complex, less rigorous than the situation they are designed to meet. If a Board of Regents, for example, represented only about one element in the population of a state, it would speak and act not only from a narrow base of support but from a limited view of wise university policy. The same would hold true for any single government bureau, or any private Board from only one background. The very disagreements over basic decisions that at times hamper us in the United States are also a source of strength, because they result from the interaction of divergent points of view. They are our best safeguard against simple tables of priority, wholesale exclusion of students from the universities, or even to some extent determination of the future pattern of society.

The last problem can be a truly serious one. If we decide, as some countries have done, the number of young people who should be allowed a university education in the various major fields, we are in effect deciding the balance of society a generation later. Decisions of national need must constantly be made, of course; many provisions of the National Defense Education Act, for instance, were devoted to the meeting of critical shortages in graduate education. It is when they are made exclusively rather than inclusively that we need to fear them, when they solve one need by restricting the work that can be done in other areas. We want to measure ourselves in the years ahead by the sum of what we accomplish, not by what we fail to accomplish or refuse to accomplish. The types of coordinating group I have in mind would have as one major responsibility the duty, not to force a balance but to keep a balance—not to dictate, but to lend encouragement and order to our pressing needs.

To say that we cannot meet these pressing needs "exclusively" is to imply a further comment on our own attitude toward planning in the next few years. We cannot solve our problems by some general pattern of rigid selection, any more than we can solve them by setting up absolutely fixed quotas and priorities within the various divisions of our educational system. If we could, for instance, be sure about which potential undergraduates deserved the major kinds of higher education, or even which ones were sure to succeed in college at all, we might risk "absolute" selection; but none of us would dare promise the certainty which would justify so radical a change in our attitude.

One feels the extent of our commitment best, perhaps, by looking at it from the viewpoint of a system of higher education like that in Britain. Our determination to provide relatively easy admission to college then looks like what it is—not amiable slackness on our part, but a conviction that we build the best society if each of us has a chance to push his intellectual talents to their reasonable limit. We cannot shift this conviction about higher education without scrapping a whole complex of beliefs.

We are likely to proceed, then, on the basic faith that we will not give up our convictions about the democracy of talent, and about the responsibility that we have to protect it and give it adequate support. As we give that support, we must remember that there is one absolutely critical difference between a program of welfare, agriculture, or flood-relief aid, and a program of aid to education. In Chapter 4 it was suggested, and quite rightly, that more complex needs in the country call for more sophisticated and at the same time standardized ways of meeting them. Granting the fact that this has often happened in other fields, we must remember that education is concerned primarily with freeing and directing the mind's creative powers, and only then, only in that major setting, with the doing of its myriad specific or vocational jobs. If we merely needed to give so many millions of students a specified amount of information, there would certainly be simpler and easier ways of doing it than those that the modern university now employs. If we mean, on the other hand, to discover and encourage the basic talents in them that they and their society will depend on in the next generation, then we have a task of human development which cannot be casually assigned even to the best bureau or the most effective committee.

Within this understanding, we must define and bring to life a way of meeting our national duty toward education. Our attitude must be protective as well as effective; it must shield the best kind of education from decisions about the use of resources that would hamper, standardize or downgrade it. To put the matter in another way, we must find a solution to our mass problem in the support of higher education without losing our sense that the individual educated person is the center of all our effort. Whatever the solution to our pressing educational needs, we must never hand over decisions about the direction of higher education to any one central committee. Centralization in this case might be just as dangerous as incoherence; and we have as much of an obligation to protect the "freedom of difference" as we do to meet the obvious and enormous needs. The ground for this attitude is not an unthinking conservatism, I believe; the task we have is simply that of ensuring an adequate future for higher education without debasing the very qualities we need most to encourage.

The Nation's Need

After we have suggested these reservations, qualifications and directions for any possible programs of future federal aid, we should perhaps recognize in the conclusion to this book our present urgent need as well as our present condition. We have certainly not found the answer to the problems of complex interaction between the federal government and higher education, but we hope that we have begun to identify the difficulty.

As we see it, and as we have described it, it has these chief aspects:

a present state of national policy about higher education which calls for a great number of crucial decisions both about the colleges and about the country; a history of federal involvement in higher education dominated by a complex but in the main unrelated group of legislative decisions; a series of programs which often give undeniable service to society while at the same time they pose problems of operation and principle for higher education; and an associated group of current issues about financing our educational needs which involve the federal government as one of a number of major financial forces influencing our future.

Implicit in these chapters have been the various difficulties we must meet—difficulties which shift and range to a much greater degree than any simple financial discussion of federal aid would suggest. It is clear that we have already made a decision about federal aid itself; and we made it so casually, almost so inadvertently, that no one can assign much credit or blame for it. As a result of these prior and *ad hoc* decisions, however, we now must decide what we mean to do in the situations which have already been created, as well as those which are dictated by our future national needs.

There are two kinds of decisions which must be made about our present practice; those which affect the order and integrity of the universities and those which similarly affect the integrity of the government. On the university side we face such problems as the assignment of true cost to government projects and the guaranteeing of relevant programs— those which fit the nature of a particular department without monopolizing or distorting it. From the government's point of view, we must ask how the multitude of partial programs could be combined or even at times redirected. Our present situation, with its very heavy investment in higher education, allows us and indeed expects us to make some effective further decisions of this kind; they would bring as much order to our present relationships as we have a right to expect.

But these decisions about improvement in our present situation must be made in the context of a second major group of decisions—those designed to meet the needs of the future. We must have decisions about the national needs which may make federal aid to higher education necessary; we must have decisions about the new areas of aid which might be involved and the types of support which might be combined. We must have decisions about the types of groups and individuals who are to share both in making these decisions and in carrying them out. And we must have decisions—finally, but perhaps most basically—about the balance, proportion and purpose in higher education to which all our various kinds of aid will be directed.

In our national planning we must speak, in short, to a complex of ideas and convictions rather than to a series of crises. We have suggested in this book a number of those which seem to us most worth attention; but they are to be taken primarily as samples or examples of what might be thought and might be done. They are important here not as "answers," but only as suggestions that the chief thing we need at the moment is newness and flexibility of thought in our planning for higher education. It is quite certain that we cannot do our job adequately merely by multiplying our present faculties and facilities, merely by demanding more from the same sources which now support us. The true context for our planning about federal aid must include a recognition both of the far-reaching responsibility put upon higher education and of the new ideas which must animate it. In such a setting the questions before us will be seen as they truly are; and we shall be asking not whether we should support higher education, but for what purposes and from what sources.

In reaching this new level of understanding, we must above all protect the human richness and complexity which are the center of true education. If colleges and universities are the keepers of value as well as the keepers of knowledge, we must make sure that our provision of adequate financial support also is a provision of adequate moral support for these two purposes. Federal financial aid, like industrial, foundation and individual aid to education, will be under great strain and change in these next years. It will do us little good as a country, however, to accept the responsibility of so much effort unless we get from it an educational system strong enough, not just to do the routine jobs, but to identify, encourage, and fulfill our best purposes as a country. The issues of federal aid, and of all kinds of support for education, must be approached from this perspective if they are to be resolved. The identification of our needs will have great value for higher education; but the recognition of why our needs must be so great has value for the whole country. Our planning should not be content with less.

Final Report of the
Seventeenth American Assembly

At the close of their discussions the participants in the Seventeenth American Assembly at Arden House, Harriman, New York, May 5-8, 1960, on THE FEDERAL GOVERNMENT AND HIGHER EDUCATION, reviewed as a group the following statement. Although there was general agreement on the Final Report, it is not the practice of The American Assembly for participants to affix their signatures, and it should not be assumed that every participant necessarily subscribes to every recommendation included in the statement.

The Need and the Challenge

This nation has urgent need to know and understand the value and condition of higher education.

We Americans believe in education. But we must understand and appreciate as never before the goals, attainments and requirements of our colleges and universities.

As a people we must recognize the essential contributions of example and achievement provided by both privately and publicly sponsored institutions. We must recognize the necessary freedom of colleges and universities to pursue the goal of truth wherever it may lead. We must understand and accept the difference between equality of educational opportunity and variability of individual talent for higher education. We must recognize that expansion of educational opportunity means

193

both the improvement of educational quality of many kinds and the growth of diverse educational institutions.

American society has achieved its present position of freedom and power through the interacting initiative, labor, and faith of individuals, groups and governments. Each of these forces has an essential role in higher education. No one person or set of persons, no one organized body, no one level of government can be expected to sustain and expand the system of higher education which will be required for our national and individual well-being.

Higher education cannot attain its purposes—the growth of the individual and the expansion of knowledge for the public good—unless students and their families take their responsibility seriously. Higher education is not a universal right. It must be available primarily on the basis of talent and interest. It must be considered a continuing challenge to the student's moral sensitivity and will to work. Students and their families must be expected to bear a part of the cost of higher education. Tuition and other fees should be increased in those institutions in which present fees are nominal or disproportionately low. A program of student aid should accompany increases in fees to assist those who cannot pay higher charges.

Equally, however, higher education needs a deep commitment from all Americans. Every citizen must realize that he shares a direct and individual responsibility not merely to sustain but actively to enhance the value in our society which only higher education can provide.

The discharge of the total responsibility for higher education requires persistently more effective management of all colleges and universities, and it calls for continued participation and increased support from individuals, corporations, foundations and all levels of government. The whole enterprise will suffer seriously if support of higher education by the federal government comes to be regarded as a substitute for other sources of support. Federal support should be only supplemental. To have it otherwise would endanger the idea of distributive responsibility which is the bedrock of effective democratic practice.

Hundreds of millions of dollars from the federal government are already flowing to colleges and universities. The amounts involved suggest great aid to higher education. This suggestion is misleading and therefore calls for critical analysis.

Present and Future Programs

There are *four general categories of federal participation* in higher education. They do not have precise boundaries, but the activities within each have similar philosophical justifications and therefore call for similar considerations as well as similar procedures and administrative treatment.

They are:

(1) Services purchased from the colleges and universities by the federal government: for example, the ROTC, the management of technological and scientific laboratories, technical assistance projects overseas, and the solution of specific problems through research and development. In these areas the government is discharging its responsibility by using the universities as means.

(2) Programs of higher education by the federal government to meet specific national needs. Examples are federal encouragement for the education of scientists, engineers, physicians, nurses, or language specialists, through scholarships, fellowships and loans to students. Such federal participation constitutes deliberate intervention for impelling national purposes.

(3) Research support by grants or contracts such as those awarded by many federal agencies to colleges and universities engaged in graduate and professional education. These programs encourage and support research both as an end in itself and as an essential means to advance education.

(4) Programs directly supporting institutions of higher education such as the appropriations to the Land-Grant institutions, loans for student housing and other income-producing buildings, and construction grants of the National Science Foundation and the National Institutes of Health.

In its estimate of national needs for higher education in the next decade, the Assembly gives emphasis to both quality and quantity. Our society demands highly educated people, in every field and in large numbers. At the same time there is an obligation to encourage the incentive of each individual, and to guarantee him the chance to develop to his full capacity. Each person, like each college or university, must have his necessary freedom of individual choice. Our colleges and universities are many and diverse, and fortunately so. They must have appropriate support without any restriction of their indispensable freedom.

In meeting its obligations to quantity, quality, and variety, higher education must as a result face these conditions: it must (a) keep its various fields and disciplines in a rational relationship with one another; (b) maintain responsibility both to the vast expansion of knowledge and the deepened moral consciousness of each educated person; (c) accomplish its ends without regimentation whether of students or teachers.

The serious difficulties which we face involve both people and money.

Enrollments are expected to double in the next ten years. Faculty salaries must be substantially increased; many kinds of education, including the costliest, must be extended; obsolescence and inadequacy of supplies, equipment and physical plant must be remedied. For these and many other reasons, the expenditure for higher education should treble.

The current shortage of competent faculty will become more acute. We must also greatly expand our facilities even with increased and more effective utilization of physical plant. Judgments and recommendations about present or future federal programs must relate to this high level of national urgency and necessity.

In meeting these responsibilities, we should maintain the well established federal tradition of making no distinction between public and private institutions. But these institutions in turn must maintain individual responsibility for their own programs; and they must demonstrate capacity and will to join together freely to guard against unnecessary restrictions or centralized control.

We wish to comment about several specific phases of current federal activities in higher education in the *four categories* mentioned above.

CATEGORY 1—SERVICES PURCHASED

In any purchase of services, the government should pay the full costs of the services it requests. There is no justification for requiring the colleges and universities to provide services to accomplish governmental ends at a financial loss to the institutions. Hence the government should negotiate contracts which include full direct and indirect costs. The colleges and universities expect no profit; they should take no loss.

CATEGORY 2—PROGRAMS OF THE FEDERAL GOVERNMENT TO MEET SPECIFIC NATIONAL NEEDS

We believe the National Defense Education Act is highly useful and should be continued beyond the expiration date of the present Act. The Act should be amended in connection with the student loan program, however, so that future teachers both in private schools and in institutions above the secondary level can have the same benefits of loan cancellation which now apply only to those who follow careers in public primary and secondary teaching.

The disclaimer affidavit required by this program is an example of unwarranted government interference in institutional policy; it should be expunged from the student loan program, and from all other federal programs which involve higher education.

We distinguish between the positive oath of loyalty and the negative disclaimer affidavit. We condemn the latter as a direct inquiry into belief, and hence contrary to the principles upon which this nation was founded. Further, this affidavit is required of college students and not of most other recipients of federal funds. In particular, the Act in no way defines or lists the subversive organizations which must be included in the affidavit; some students might in innocence join an organization which could at some future time be listed as subversive.

We must register one other objection: it is a hindrance to education to interfere with the policy of individual states, as recent National Defence Education Act legislation has done, by the direct allocation of graduate fellowships to specific institutions in violation of an agreed state plan. This is unwarranted federal trespass upon state functions.

CATEGORY 3—SUPPORT OF RESEARCH

Federal grants for research, which loom so large in many university budgets, should include the full indirect cost of conducting the program. These grants further the purposes of the institution itself, and thus are not wholly parallel to the purchase of services for a government purpose. However, such programs inevitably tend to create some imbalance and distortion in the operation of the institution, and if the institution is in addition compelled to divert its own funds to their support, these adverse effects become excessive. Only if government assumes the full cost is the balance between benefit and interference an equitable one.

CATEGORY 4—PROGRAMS DIRECTLY SUPPORTING INSTITUTIONS OF HIGHER EDUCATION

We approve and endorse the practice of the National Science Foundation and the National Institutes of Health in making funds available for research facilities appropriate to under-graduate instruction, particularly in liberal-arts colleges. Many scholar-teachers come from these colleges, and they must not be neglected. Therefore we urge the extension of such programs.

The program of loans for college housing and other self-liquidating facilities should be continued. It should be operated on the same formula as now prevails.

A serious issue of federal action concerns the extension of direct federal support beyond these existing programs. The best available projections of total need leave serious doubt whether the required financial resources can be obtained from state and local governments, from tuition fees, and from private sources, including corporations. We urge that funds from these sources be expanded to the maximum, and repeat that no federal action should operate to discourage them. Nevertheless, the need must be met.

Programs

Of all the appropriate areas of increased federal support, the Assembly thinks that the one posing the least threat to college and to university freedom and the one most worth stressing is that of assisting with the provision of capital facilities.

We recommend that institutional aid be provided on a matching basis through a program of federal grants for construction of facilities, including libraries but excluding dormitories (which are otherwise provided for) and athletic facilities.

There is also some sentiment for direct aid to institutions for instructional purposes and direct assistance to students through federal scholarships. Careful thought must be given to both of these—the amounts of help which may be necessary and the ways in which both the colleges and the government might administer such programs. Financial assistance to institutions for instructional purposes might best be established in proportion to enrollment and on a matching basis.

Organizations

There is a definite need for one organization to coordinate the efforts of spokesmen of American higher education to speak on the national level on the issues about which all institutions are concerned. The American Council on Education could serve this purpose. The colleges and universities of the country must, however, take the major initiative in guaranteeing the accomplishment of this essential job. First they must take the responsibility of defending their own freedom, and this will make possible the fusing of their collective efforts for freedom within the structure of the American Council on Education.

There should be a private and unofficial body designed to keep constantly before the public the importance of maintaining vigorous institutions of higher education, and of encouraging the support of education by public opinion. This non-governmental citizens' committee for higher education should take as its major function the interpretation to the country of the achievements and the urgent needs of its many and diverse institutions of higher education.

Education is a vast and a vital national concern. The President, the Congress and the public should have up-to-date, frequent, regular, and authoritative official information. To achieve this there is a need for a Council of Advisors on Education in the office of the President. It should be established by law and perform a function analogous to that of the Council of Economic Advisors. This Council should make an annual report to the President on education—its advances, its deficiencies and its needs. It should lay adequate stress upon higher education, which is becoming increasingly important to the national welfare. The report of this Council, like the report of the Council of Economic Advisors, should also be transmitted to a joint committee of the Congress which would hold hearings upon it, in order to reach conclusions and draft its own reports.

Participants in the Seventeenth American Assembly

ROBERT C. ANDERSON
Director
Southern Regional Education
  Board
Atlanta

NORMAN P. AUBURN
President
The University of Akron
Ohio

P. MILO BAIL
Chairman
Commission on Colleges and
  Universities
North Central Association of Col-
  leges and Secondary Schools
Omaha

WILLIAM BENTON
Publisher
Encyclopaedia Britannica
Connecticut

BUFORD BOONE
Publisher
The Tuscaloosa News
Alabama

JOHN W. BOWEN
Major General, U.S.A.
Asst. Chief of Staff for Reserve
  Components
Washington, D. C.

JOHN BRADEMAS
Representative from Indiana
Congress of the United States

PAUL J. BRAISTED
President
The Edward W. Hazen Founda-
  tion
New Haven

COURTNEY C. BROWN
Dean
Graduate School of Business
Columbia University

200

WILLIAM P. BUNDY
Staff Director
The President's Commission on
National Goals
Washington, D. C.

A. BOYD CAMPBELL
President
Mississippi School Supply Company
Jackson

JOSEPH S. CLARK
United States Senator from
Pennsylvania

CATHERINE B. CLEARY
Vice President
First Wisconsin Trust Company
Milwaukee

JAMES S. COLES
President
Bowdoin College
Maine

L. V. COLLINGS
Chairman
Standard-Vacuum Oil Company
White Plains, New York

JOHN D. CONNORS
Director of Education
AFL-CIO
Washington, D. C.

H. H. DEWAR
Member, Board of Governors
New York Stock Exchange
San Antonio

PETER O. DIETZ
Harriman Scholar
Columbia University

THEODORE A. DISTLER
Executive Director
Association of American Colleges
Washington, D. C.

MARRINER S. ECCLES
Chairman
First Security Corporation
Salt Lake City

JOHN R. ELLIOTT
Harriman Scholar
Columbia University

CLARENCE H. FAUST
President
The Fund for the Advancement of
Education
New York City

WILLIAM C. FELS
President
Bennington College
Vermont

SIDNEY F. GIFFIN
Brigadier General, USAF
Director
Office of Armed Forces Information and Education
Department of Defense
Washington, D. C.

MRS. CARL J. GILBERT
Dover, Massachusetts

A. CRAWFORD GREENE
McCutcheon, Thomas Matthew,
Griffiths & Greene
San Francisco

REUBEN H. GROSS
Associate
A Study of the American High
School
New York City

RALPH S. HALFORD
Vice Provost
Columbia University

SEYMOUR E. HARRIS
Professor of Political Economy
Harvard University

FRANK N. HAWKINS
Associate Editor
Pittsburgh *Post-Gazette* &
  Sun-Telegraph
Pennsylvania

ERNEST V. HOLLIS
Director
College and University Adminis-
  tration Branch
Division of Higher Education
Dept. of Health, Education and
  Welfare
Washington, D. C.

JOHN C. HONEY
Executive Associate
Carnegie Corporation of New York

MORRIS IUSHEWITZ
Secretary
The New York City Central Labor
  Council
AFL-CIO

JOHN ERIK JONSSON
Chairman
Texas Instruments, Inc.
Dallas

ALLAN B. KLINE
Western Springs, Illinois

DOUGLAS M. KNIGHT
President
Lawrence College
Wisconsin

J. KENNETH LITTLE
Director
Survey of Federal Programs in
  Higher Education
Dept. of Health, Education and
  Welfare
Washington, D. C.

HERBERT E. LONGENECKER
President
Tulane University
New Orleans

THE MOST REVEREND
  J. M. MARLING
Bishop of Jefferson City
Missouri

JOHN H. MARTIN
President
United Lumber Yards
Modesto, California

JAMES McCORMACK, JR.
Vice President
Massachusetts Institute of Tech-
  nology

EUGENE McELVANEY
Senior Vice President
First National Bank in Dallas
Texas

FRANK E. McGINITY
Harriman Scholar
Columbia University

JOHN D. MILLETT
President
Miami University
Ohio

JOHN S. MILLIS
President
Western Reserve University
Cleveland

MALCOLM MUIR
Chairman & Publisher
Newsweek
New York City

GARRISON NORTON
President
Institute for Defense Analyses
Washington, D. C.

THOMAS PARRAN
President
Avalon Foundation
New York City

JOHN A. PERKINS
President
University of Delaware

THE REVEREND CANON
J. W. PYLE
The Cathedral Church of St. John
the Divine
New York City

VERY REVEREND
P.C. REINERT
President
St. Louis University
Missouri

JOHN W. ROLLINS
Chairman
Rollins Leasing Corporation
Wilmington

HAROLD S. SHEFELMAN,
Weter, Roberts & Shefelman
Seattle

G. KERRY SMITH
Executive Secretary
Association for Higher Education
Washington, D. C.

FRANK H. SPARKS
President
Council for Financial Aid to
Education, Inc.
New York City

J. E. WALLACE STERLING
President
Stanford University
California

W. S. STONE
Major General, USAF
Superintendent
United States Air Force Academy
Colorado

RUSSELL I. THACKREY
Executive Secretary
American Association of Land-
Grant Colleges and State Uni-
versities
Washington, D. C.

CHARLES E. THWAITE, JR.
Chairman
Trust Company of Georgia
Atlanta

DENNIS N. WARTERS
President
Bankers Life Company
Des Moines

ALAN T. WATERMAN
Director
National Science Foundation
Washington, D. C.

The American Assembly

S*ince its establishment by Dwight D. Eisenhower at Columbia University in 1950, the American Assembly has held assemblies of national leaders and has published books to illuminate issues of United States policy.*

The Assembly is a national, non-partisan, educational institution, incorporated under the State of New York.

The Trustees of the Assembly approve a topic for presentation in a background book, authoritatively designed and written to aid deliberations at national Assembly sessions at Arden House, the Harriman Campus of Columbia University. These books are also used to support discussion at regional Assembly sessions and to evoke consideration by the general public.

All sessions of the Assembly, whether national or local, issue and publicize independent reports of conclusions and recommendations on the topic at hand. Participants in these sessions constitute a wide range of experience and competence.

The American Assembly is the administrator of the President's Commission on National Goals, which was appointed by President Eisenhower in January, 1960.

The following institutions have cooperated with the Assembly in sponsoring regional, state or municipal sessions across the country:

Stanford University
University of California (Berkeley)
University of California (Los Angeles)
University of Wyoming
University of Denver
University of New Mexico
University of Oklahoma
Dallas Council on World Affairs
The Rice Institute
Tulane University
Southwestern at Memphis
Duke University
University of Florida
Emory University
University of Illinois
Minnesota World Affairs Center
University of Washington
University of Puerto Rico
Lawrence College

Cleveland Council on World Affairs
University of Missouri
Washington University
Drake University
Indiana University
University of Vermont
Tufts University
Foreign Policy Association of Pittsburgh
Southern Methodist University
University of Texas
Town Hall of Los Angeles
North Central Association
United States Air Force Academy
University of Arkansas
Michigan State University
Kansas City International Relations
  Council
Vanderbilt University
University of Arizona

American Assembly books are purchased and put to use by thousands of individuals, libraries, businesses, public agencies, non-governmental organizations, educational institutions, discussion meetings and service groups. *The subjects of Assembly studies to date are:*

1960—THE FEDERAL GOVERNMENT AND HIGHER
EDUCATION

> *Library, cloth bound edition, $3.50*
> *Spectrum, paper bound edition, $1.95*
> *Available from better booksellers and Prentice-Hall, Inc.*

The following titles were published by the American Assembly. Prices indicate books which can be obtained by writing to The American Assembly.

1959—THE UNITED STATES AND LATIN AMERICA ($2.00)
—WAGES, PRICES, PROFITS AND PRODUCTIVITY ($2.00)

1958—THE UNITED STATES AND AFRICA ($2.00)
—UNITED STATES MONETARY POLICY ($2.00)

1957—ATOMS FOR POWER ($1.00)
—INTERNATIONAL STABILITY AND PROGRESS

1956—THE UNITED STATES AND THE FAR EAST
—THE REPRESENTATION OF THE UNITED STATES
ABROAD

1955—THE FORTY-EIGHT STATES
—UNITED STATES AGRICULTURE

1954—THE FEDERAL GOVERNMENT SERVICE ($1.00)
—THE UNITED STATES STAKE IN THE UNITED NATIONS

1953—ECONOMIC SECURITY FOR AMERICANS

1952—INFLATION

1951—UNITED STATES-WESTERN EUROPE RELATIONSHIPS

Regular readers of the American Assembly receive early copies of each new Assembly study and are billed subsequently. To enroll as a regular reader, or for additional information, please address:

The American Assembly, Columbia University, New York 27, New York.

Future Assembly books, to be published by Prentice-Hall, Inc., are:

—THE SECRETARY OF STATE
—ARMS LIMITATION AND THE PUBLIC